Good Night Irene

Stories and photos about the tropical storm that devastated Vermont, the Catskills and the Berkshires

Craig Brandon
Nicole Garman
Michael Ryan

Good Night Irene:
Stories and photos about the tropical storm
that devastated Vermont, the Catskills and the Berkshires

By
Craig Brandon
Nicole Garman
Michael Ryan
edited by Craig Brandon

ISBN: 978-0-9829853-2-8
First Edition

QC984N35
974.2 BRA

Cataloging Information:
AUTHOR: Brandon, Craig AUTHOR: Garman, Nicole AUTHOR:
Ryan, Michael TITLE: Good Night Irene: Stories and Photos about
the tropical storm that devastated Vermont, the Catskills and The
Berkshires
p. cm.
Includes Index
1. Natural Disasters - New England - History; 2 Natural Disasters
- New York State - History; 3. Natural Disasters - Massachusetts -
History

Cover photo: Evelyn Rikard, Ella Tree and Dave Rikard of Prattsville, New York,
watch as an excavator destroys the remains of their house, which was severely
damaged by Tropical Storm Irene. Photo by Hans Pennink (FEMA)

Surry Cottage Books
800 Park Avenue
Keene NH 03431
(603) 499-6500
www.surrycottagebooks.com

*To the resilient residents of the Irene Zone, who
endured unspeakable losses during eight hours on
August 28, 2011,
but who stood firm
in their commitment to their towns,
their friends and their communities.*

The Irene Zone

Table of Contents

Preface

By Philip Cabot Camp Sr.

Good Night Irene provides insight into much more than just the destruction of homes, businesses, roads, bridges and personal property wrought by Tropical Storm Irene. Equally important, it speaks to the resiliency and selflessness of people in Vermont, the Catskills and the Berkshires who faced and overcame a crisis of enormous proportions.

Having lived in Vermont my entire life, I thought that I'd witnessed about all there was to know about how special Vermonters are. I was wrong.

In the aftermath of one of Vermont's most punishing natural disasters, no one escaped the emotional or economic hardships created by Irene. Even so, it triggered something positive and good in virtually everyone, whether they were directly or indirectly affected by the crisis.

I was there, knee-deep in rapidly rising floodwaters that were sweeping lifelong memories downriver and across fields, destroying miles of roads, ripping bridges from their foundations and destroying the beautiful countryside that was preparing to welcome the annual pilgrimage of visitors coming to view fall foliage.

With floodwaters still draining from the building that had housed my newspaper business, they came. My staff, neighbors, friends from afar and a few people I'd never met before. Out of nowhere they came to see what they could do to help me. I didn't ask anyone to help, they just arrived and pitched in. Scenes like this were common throughout the region.

Every community needs things to inspire its citizens and to bring out the best in individuals, if it is to be a peaceful, successful, happy place. Irene did this, and in spades. Those communities impacted by Irene are coming back, and most will be better than ever. People have experienced the thrill of extraordinary community spirit, the comforting feeling of common purpose and the knowledge that adversity can be overcome when people work together.

Thousands of stories about Irene and the disaster will be told in books, speeches, community meetings, in coffee shops and around campfires by people who witnessed the devastation and recovery. This book, *Good Night Irene*, is not only a must-read, but also a must share. Keep it in plain sight, where it can easily be shared with others. ๙

Philip Cabot Camp Sr. is a native Vermonter who spent a career in the ski industry before purchasing the Vermont Standard, *the state's oldest weekly newspaper and serving as its publisher. His own experience with Irene is described in Chapter 7.*

Introduction
Eight hours on an August Sunday

The terrible destruction described in this book took place in a mere eight hours on Sunday August 28, 2011, beginning as early as 10 a.m. in some places and not until later at night in others. After those eight hours, the water began to recede, and it was only then that the true extent of the disaster was understood. As this book goes to press, six months after the disaster, recovery has begun, but it will take years of work before the eight communities described in detail in this book can return to anything like "normal."

In the week after the storm, stories began to emerge not only about the devastation but also amazing tales of rescues, about people helping their neighbors, about survivors who lost their homes and all their personal belongings yet vowed to rebuild, no matter what the cost.

As a book publisher and author, I could see a terrible, dramatic yet wonderful story to be told. The idea for this book dates back to Labor Day weekend 2011 in a Brattleboro Thai restaurant and a conversation with my friend Ed Smith, an Amherst, Massachusetts attorney. When he casually asked me what I was up to, I told him about a vague notion for a book about Tropical Storm Irene. For a small, regional publisher like Surry Cottage Books, capturing a multiple-state story like this would be a major undertaking. How could we tell it?

The original idea was much bigger and would have included New Jersey and Connecticut as well as the three states we eventually chose. It would have taken me at least a year to visit all those places, interview survivors and collect photos. "But why do you have to do it yourself?" Ed asked. "There must be hundreds of unemployed former journalists out there. What if you hired one for each town?"

Freelancers responded enthusiastically to the idea, and I was overwhelmed with responses. Many of these writers wanted $5,000 to write 5000 words and since I needed twelve writers that would be a bill of a mere $60,000! Similarly, professional photographers wanted $500 per picture and I needed 200 pictures. That would be another $100,000. I could charge $500 a copy and still not break even!

So I dug a little deeper and found some unemployed writers and photographers willing to work at prices I could afford. I selected a half dozen who lived near the Irene-impacted areas and gave them the assignment: talk with everybody, get lots of photos and send me 5,000 words by February. Each of them signed a contract and agreed to a deadline.

Easy! But it turned out to be too easy. The deadline came and went and no one sent me anything. Not one word. Some simply refused to return my messages and calls. Others promised to send me the story "tomorrow," which turned into weeks and finally months. Of the half dozen freelancers only Nicole Garman in central Vermont remained. It looked for a time like the whole project was in jeopardy.

When the Catskills writer didn't send anything a month after deadline, I went looking for an emergency replacement and found Mike Ryan of the *Catskill Daily Mail*, who jumped right in, sent me his copy in two weeks and saved the entire project.

It turned out we couldn't do twelve towns with any kind of depth and still have a reasonably sized book, so we reduced the number of towns we could cover. The final eight were chosen not because they were the most damaged towns but because they had the most interesting stories to tell.

All three of us are happy with the results of our work and hope you will be as well. It was the most complicated project Surry Cottage Books had ever attempted, with lots of logistical problems, but all three of us feel this book will serve a dual purpose: to tell the stories of courageous survivors and to create a historic record of an important event. As you read the stories about the incredible destruction, the broken lives and the terrible cost, it's nearly impossible to believe that all this damage took place in just eight hours on August 28. It's an incredible statement about the power of nature. We hope you enjoy reading it as much as we enjoyed researching, photographing and writing it. ◄

- Craig Brandon
Publisher

1
Birth of a Monster

Born in Africa, a killer storm stalks the East Coast
with her eye set on New York and New England

The sun shower that was destined to become the killer storm Irene took its first breath on a quiet August afternoon in the Ethiopian Highlands just north of the capital city of Addis Ababa and east of lake T'ana Hayk, the source of the Blue Nile. A small area of low pressure with clouds barely large enough to be visible from satellite weather cameras, it produced some cloudiness and perhaps a gentle shower as it slowly drifted toward the west at a few miles per hour. Meanwhile, 6,800 miles away in what was to become the Irene Zone, no one showed the slightest interest in it.

As it crossed the Sahara Desert over the next few days, pushed along by the variable winds of the Intertropical Convergence Zone, it picked up energy from the extremely hot sands and rock that had been baking in the bright sunlight all summer. The Sahara, the largest desert in the world, is about the size of the United States and most of it lies within the so-called Horse Latitudes, an area of light winds and dry weather. A column of hot air known as the African Easterly Jet picked up the air mass and pulled it three miles above the sand and rock, until the very dry winds of infant and yet unnamed Irene

Photo: NASA

Irene as a category 3 hurricane over the Bahamas on August 24, 2011.

reached the coast of Morocco on August 15, 2011, where the dry, thirsty winds immediately set about sucking up moisture from the Atlantic Ocean. The flow of the ocean combined with the spin of the Earth created a gentle turning, forcing the winds of the infant Irene to flow counterclockwise, or widdershins, as witches call this turning in what they consider an unnatural or satanic direction.

Meteorologists at the National Hurricane Center in Miami immediately took notice of her. While most of the tropical waves that enter the Atlantic from Morocco disperse within a few days, veteran hurricane hunters understood immediately that this storm was unusually wide and had all the makings of a killer.

As it passed to the south of the Cape Verde Islands, however, the storm failed to develop the kinds of thunderstorms that meteorologists expected, and it remained spread out over a large area rather that circulating around a set point to create an "eye."

On August 19, now over the eastern Atlantic, the atmospheric pressure around the storm dropped and the rotation became more pronounced. Ahead of her was a mass of very warm water that was ideal for hurricane formation. The next day, as the storm reached the Lesser Antilles, the National Hurricane Center announced that the storm was about to become a cyclone, and a reconnaissance plane found a small surface circulation center and unusually high winds. At 11 p.m. the Hurricane Center announced that the wave had developed into a tropical storm and finally gave her a name: Irene, the ninth named storm of the 2011 season.

"Irene" is a woman's name that originated with the Greek name, εἰρήνη (eiréné), which ironically means "peace." The 2011 storm was not the first one to use the name. There had already been five other hurricanes and two tropical storms dating back to 1947, but none of them had been considered powerful enough to retire the name. That allowed the 2011 killer to use the name, which has now been officially retired, meaning there will never again be a storm with her name.

The first tropical storm watches were sent out the next day, August 20, and two days later Irene made her first landfall at Punta Santiago in Puerto Rico as a Category 1 hurricane. She became a killer when a driver was caught in a swollen river and died, becoming the first of 54 people to die at the hands of Irene. Banana plantations were destroyed and peak winds at higher elevations were measured at 111 miles per hour. From there, Irene tracked north near the Dominican Republic, where she caused heavy rains, flash floods and more deaths. On August 24, Irene passed over the Turks and Caicos Islands, where she blew the roofs off houses and then passed through the Bahamas with wind gusts recorded at 140 miles per hour

Nearing the coast of the United States, Irene finally developed the characteristic "eye," formation, the clear area around the center of rotation as she intensified into a Category 3 hurricane.

At 7:30 a.m. on August 27, after weakening back to a Category 1 with winds of 85 miles per hour, Irene made her first American landfall at Cape Lookout, North Carolina and spawned tornadoes inland. Just ten hours later she was back over the Atlantic and just before sunrise the next day, Sunday, August 28 she made another landfall at Little Egg Inlet in New Jersey, where winds of 75 miles per hour were recorded. When Irene drifted back over the ocean again, her wind speeds dropped to under 65 miles per hour and she was downgraded to a tropical storm again.

By now, people in the Irene Zone were taking serious notice. The projected track of the storm had her roaring inland and turning north up the Hudson River Valley. The national news media, which had been covering the winds and storm surge extensively for days, noted that the storm was scheduled to pass over New York City, but as the wind speeds dropped and the storm became less concentrated, the news crews went home, telling viewers that the Irene story was over because New York suffered only minor damage.

Later that day, as the disorganized tropical storm moved north, roughly tracing the eastern shore of the Hudson Valley, residents who had been making preparations for a hurricane began to relax. The winds had diminished and Irene was now "only" a tropical storm, so what was there to worry about? Many thought they had dodged the bullet.

Meanwhile, rain began to fall in a 40,000-square-mile area from Maine to the Catskills and from the Berkshires to the White Mountains: the Irene Zone. There's no evidence that the intensity of Irene's rainfall increased at this point. In fact, it seemed to be diminishing, like the winds. But as the storm lost its momentum, slowing down its journey to the north, it took a deep breath, like a jogger winded from a tough uphill climb. The intense levels of rain that had been spread out over a wide area while Irene was moving now sat down over the Irene Zone area for seven to eight hours, opening the floodgates. Throughout the morning and into the afternoon, the rain was relentless as Irene dumped the millions of pounds of water she had accumulated over the Atlantic onto the mountains of New England and New York. The hillsides, already saturated from previous storms, couldn't absorb any more water and so, carried by gravity, the water

Did a 1991 movie predict Irene?

*E*ven before Hurricane
Irene first made landfall in
North Carolina, Internet
*bloggers made an interesting
connection. Had the hurricane
been predicted in the 1991 film
"The Addams Family"?*

*In a scene near the end of the
movie, Uncle Fester, the zombie-
like, pale-faced ghoul played
by Christopher Lloyd, is having
a dispute with his adopted
mother and her lawyer. He walks
over to a wall filled with books
and chooses one clearly marked
"Hurricane Irene." When he
opens it, there are lightning flashes, and winds swirl around
the room coming from the palm trees swaying in the book. The
mother and her lawyer are blown away into the sky and then
into their graves.*

*It wasn't long until bloggers were writing about this as a
conspiracy concocted by the Illuminati as a secret warning. It
was, of course, nothing but a coincidence, right?*

*But, then again, Hurricane Irene was also the name of a
storm in the movie "Deep Impact." Maybe Irene was just an
element in a script writers' plot list. Who knows?* ✍

began to move downhill, heading for small towns that were
mostly unprepared for what was about to happen.

Many residents said their first indication that something
unusual was happening were the sounds of thumping boulders
being carried downstream in what had been scenic, babbling
brooks. Others said it was the sound of large trees snapping in half
as their roots loosened in the soil. Still others didn't understand

Photo: Craig Brandon
The remains of a home in Wardsboro, Vermont, destroyed by floods caused by Tropical Storm Irene.

what was happening until their houses began to shift as raging water attacked their homes' foundations, causing their timbers to snap and moan. Those keeping a close watch on their streams and rivers watched them rise, slowly at first and then suddenly rising seven or eight feet in a single hour: a flash flood.

What they were experiencing was what meteorologists call a "five-hundred-year flood," one that occurs roughly twice a millennium. In New England, that meant the last one had probably occurred before the Pilgrims landed. While a normal nor'easter was like a garden hose, dumping two inches of rain over a 24-hour period, Irene was more like a fire hose, flowing at a rate of two inches per hour for seven hours, or five to eight inches of rain over Vermont and as much as 17 inches over the Catskills. Two months of rain fell in just a few hours, and the inevitable result of all that rain was a tidal wave of water that grew in intensity as it rushed down the mountainsides, pulled by gravity, removing anything in its path: trees, houses, boulders, propane tanks, cars, bridges and highways — all became part of the shock wave with the force of a battering ram.

Thomas Zimmie, professor of civil engineering at Rensselaer Polytechnic Institute in Troy, New York, said topography was destiny in the Irene Zone. When heavy rains fall on flat land, he said, the water spreads out and runs off in all directions. But when heavy rains fall at the tops of mountains, the water picks up speed and energy as it descends, like what happens on a tilted roof. All that water races down to the gutters and then increases in intensity as it runs into the downspouts. The mountain streams of the Catskills and Green Mountains became the downspouts that concentrated and intensified the power of all that water.

Small streams became raging torrents as they gathered momentum in their rush downstream at ten times their normal flow and intensity. One gallon of water weighs 8.3 pounds, and Irene had picked up millions of gallons in her journey over the Atlantic, dumping much of it on the Irene Zone. Flash floods moved downhill, increasing in intensity as they tried to pass within their old stream beds, headed straight for the communities built next to them.

The result was more destructive than an earthquake. Residents of Wilmington, Prattsville, Waterbury and Schoharie watched helplessly as the wall of water tore buildings to pieces and turned main streets into white-water rafting courses. While some parts of towns were merely flooded as calm water seeped under doors into basements, other areas suffered direct hits from the wall of water, crashing through at a high rate of speed, carrying along anything in its path. But the water wasn't white; it was chocolate brown, filled with the valuable topsoil it stole from uphill farms.

Roadways that ran next to these raging rivers and brooks were not just flooded but actively eroded as the waterways widened their paths in an effort to accommodate the flow, undermining the adjacent land and collapsing the guardrails and eventually the pavement into the deluge. Culverts that were never designed for this kind of abuse became clogged, and the water rushed over the top of the pavement.

Bridges that spanned these raging brooks had their abutments

Photo: Angela Drexel (FEMA)
Main Street, Brandon, Vermont, after Irene.

eroded from both sides until the span had nothing to rest on and crashed into the river. In some cases, houses that had been dislodged floated downstream in the flood and crashed into the bridges, weakening their attachment to their abutments and pushing them into the river.

The actual flash flood did not last long. In most places the wall of rushing water subsided within a few hours, earlier in some places and later in others. Residents of the Irene Zone didn't grasp the full measure of the devastation until they awoke on Monday morning to life in a disaster zone. It was a bright sunny day with clear blue skies, as if Irene were only a bad dream. Dozens of communities in Vermont and the Catskills were shut off from the rest of the world, without electricity, telephones or running water. A combination of bridge collapses and road washouts meant there was no way in or out of town. Instead of going to their jobs, survivors began the process of digging out, helping rescue their neighbors and building temporary bridges so emergency crews and trucks carrying food and water could get in and the sick and injured could be taken to area hospitals. Medical helicopters were called into isolated communities like Rochester and Wilmington to remove patients.

The national news media, which had gone home when Irene failed to inflict much damage in New York City, was slow to wake up to the fact that a major storm story was in progress in Vermont and the Catskills, areas far away from the ocean and not part of the planned coverage zone. Newspapers could not be delivered to the worst-hit areas, and in Woodstock, Vermont, the local weekly itself was flooded out of its offices. Radio stations took over to inform residents about how bad it was, while bloggers and social media sent news from inside the isolated areas, where residents had no other way of knowing if help was on the way. Land lines were down and cell phones went dead when their towers lost power or were washed away. A major source of news was YouTube, which showed dozens of amateur videos of towns being destroyed and the ruins that remained.

During the day on Monday, August 29, awestruck residents explored their new world, which bore little resemblance to what it had been just a day before. Business owners returned to their shops to find windows broken, walls smashed and inventory spread out along the street and down the local waterway. Left behind was a thick layer of shiny, slippery, smelly mud with the consistency and color of chocolate pudding, full of sewage,

Photo: Angela Drexel (FEMA)

Brandon, Vermont, after Irene.

farm chemicals, heating oil and leaking propane tanks. Even spectators standing on what they thought was the newly formed shore weren't safe as banks collapsed and washed them and their cars into the raging torrent. In Rochester, Vermont, a small stream that had been transformed by Irene into a monster eroded a trench through a century-old cemetery, uncovering caskets and corpses and floating them down Route 100.

The draining of towns like Brattleboro, Prattsville, Schoharie, Wilmington, Rochester and Waterbury revealed the full extent of the damage. While some residents gave up in despair, vowing they would never be able to recover, most stayed, determined to rebuild and helping their neighbors clean out the water-damaged furniture and store fixtures, using sledge hammers to tear the sheetrock from walls to prevent mold, hiring water damage cleanup companies to bring in industrial-sized dehumidifiers and hiring engineers to look at damaged foundations to see if rebuilding was even possible. The results could be seen even from outer space as the mud deposited by Irene fanned out into Long Island Sound at the mouth of the Connecticut River.

While there were few deaths and officials tried to put a price tag on the billions of dollars in damage, there was no way to calculate the psychological toll that had been inflicted on residents of the Irene Zone. How do you recover from watching your home and your belongings torn apart and floated away by a raging river? How do you recover when a life's worth of artwork is swept away? How do you recover when all your belongings have to be thrown away because they came in contact with six inches of toxic mud? How do you regain your courage when the business you worked so hard to establish is suddenly gone?

In the chapters that follow, this book will tell the stories of the survivors who lost everything and then, with the help of their neighbors and friends, found ways to go on with their lives in a landscape that might require decades to recover from the damage of just eight hours on August 28, 2011. ◄

2
The Day of the Disaster

A Sunday tour slowly reveals the extent of the damage and how much of the world has changed.

By Luke Q. Stafford

It began as a routine Sunday morning. Hurricane Irene had been weakened to "Tropical Storm" Irene the night before, so we didn't think anything of the steady rain pattering on our roof as my wife fixed coffee and I fed our infant daughter mashed pears. I was excited to have a gray, rainy day as an excuse to lie around and catch up on preseason football news.

I drained my second cup of coffee while issuing smart-ass remarks to TV news reporters as they admitted overestimating Irene's impact on New York City.

"I can't believe they shut down the entire city for this," smirked my wife. "Yeah, Jim Cantore is a crock," I quipped.

As CBS Morning News was starting, I heard thunder. Unlike thunder, though, the ground was shaking with each rumble. "What the. . . ?" I muttered to myself. I walked out the front door to see what I could see. What I saw didn't necessarily frighten me, but it did cause me to stare in disbelief for a few moments. The Rock River, a normally placid brook across the road from our house, where we bring our daughter for afternoon dips, was a swiftly moving mass of chocolate-brown water. I threw

Photo: Luke Q. Stafford
Dover Road, South Newfane, Vermont, on August 29.

on a jacket and walked a few hundred feet up to the Parish Hill bridge, pulling out my cell phone to record the furious torrent below me. The rumble I'd heard? There were boulders crashing into each other deep below the swirling surface, the river tossing them like pebbles.

Our neighbors from across the road pulled into the driveway next door. "That's weird," I thought. I knocked on the door to see what was up. The river had reached their house, the neighbors across the road said. It happened in a matter of minutes. They were coming to higher ground. By this time, entire trees—roots, leaves and all—were floating by. I was starting to regret making fun of all those weather reporters. Even more, I was regretting my decision to refuse flood insurance from the mortgage company.

"Pack some bags," I directed my wife, trying to maintain calm in my voice.

"What's going . . ."

"Just pack clothes and a laptop," I interrupted.

We evacuated as the Rock River crested Dover Road. We made it safely into Brattleboro. For the next three hours, the river raged and flailed and clawed at its banks, sweeping away houses and carrying huge chunks of road down to the Connecticut River. It devoured vehicles, scarred mountainsides and brought utility poles crashing down. It spared some homes and swallowed up others. As darkness fell, the water receded, and the photos of the damage began to surface online. I slept little that night, wondering how I was going to shelter my family if I no longer had a home.

We returned 24 hours after we left, the sun now shining and the birds chirping. We crossed the bridge where I had stood with my cell phone a day earlier. At the other side, we climbed a ladder to get back to road level; the bridge's foundation had given way, dropping it six feet on one side. Our house was still standing, but the river had carved away the earth in front of it, taking the road with it. Miraculously, the section of carved earth stopped about 20 feet from our front door. A neighbor just down the road was not so lucky. The Rock River was now gently flowing where his house once stood. The bottom floor of his house had disintegrated, but the top floor was eerily intact, 300 yards away.

The story was the same all over Vermont. Hundred-yard-long, 15-foot-deep chasms had bitten into roadways from Waterbury to Bennington, Brattleboro to Rutland. At Okemo Mountain, ac-

Photo: Luke Q. Stafford

National Guard soldiers patrol a flooded street in Brattleboro.

cess roads washed away and the marketing offices were flooded. A section of foundation at Killington mountain's base lodge succumbed to rushing water, causing the Superstar Pub to dislodge from its host building. In Wilmington, a crossroads town 15 minutes south of Mount Snow, a woman was swept away in rising waters and later found dead along the shores of the Deerfield River. She was a housekeeper at Mount Snow, here from Macedonia on a work program.

Some small towns found themselves completely cut off from the rest of the world when the sun rose Monday morning, August 29. Power and phone lines were severed (cell signals were mostly nonexistent in these small mountain towns even before the storm). Vehicles could not leave or enter. The only way to check on neighbors in some remote locations was to hike on foot, bushwacking through underbrush to get around washed-out sections of road.

I spent the afternoon walking around with a camera, feeling like a protagonist in a Cormac McCarthy novel. I was documenting the destruction for a Facebook page I'd already planned to create to help the community stay informed and updated in the chaotic days that surely lay ahead. I expected to find crying children and men with their heads in their hands, to come upon distraught homeowners dumbfounded and heartbroken. But I found nothing like that.

Instead of forlorn individuals crying on their doorsteps, I found next-door neighbors hugging each other and laughing. There were no weeping children, but there were friendly folks helping each other pump out flooded basements. That evening, my next-door neighbor invited everyone in the neighborhood to a "clean out your freezer" barbeque, where smiles outnumbered frowns a thousand to one. State Senator Peter Galbraith even showed up, assuring us that Vermont would rebound.

"That's what Vermonters do," said Bonnie MacPherson, director of public relations at Okemo Mountain Resort. "They are resilient in the face of adversity."

With her offices flooded, lifts damaged, and access roads washed away, MacPherson immediately started to look for ways to help the community at large. She helped organize and run "Vermont Will Rise Again," a benefit concert at Jackson Gore that

Photo: Luke Q. Stafford

Residents use a ladder to climb up onto the Parish Hill bridge in South Newfane to get across.

was free to all, but accepted donations that would go directly to valley residents affected by Irene's floods.

The softer side of Vermonters was bursting forth all across the state. National media couldn't help but cover the "neighbor helping neighbor" angle of the story, as that was all Green Mountain Staters seemed to answer when asked, "What's it like in Vermont right now?"

But as the initial shock of the destruction wore off, the tough side of Vermont was peeking through as well. "If the resort had snow, we would be open with the K-1 Lodge providing all normal skier services, minus one bar," said Sarah Thorson, communications manager at Killington Resort, assuring us that, even though a wing of the base lodge was out of commission, it wasn't going to stop them from providing skiers and riders with the full Killington experience. "We still plan to be one of the first resorts to open on the East Coast."

All told, Vermont's ski resorts were in surprisingly great shape, considering the destruction wrought on low-lying hamlets across the state. Stratton Mountain posted a photo of blooming daisies and lush, green trails on its website two days after the flooding, telling the world, "we're open for business." Stowe posted a blog titled "Come in! We're open!"noting that the "roads are clear, attractions are open and the first hints of color are painting the trees."

It's one week after the great flood of 2011, and my wife and I are amazed to have electricity restored to our home, even though the utility pole across from our house is lying on its side, partially submerged in water and surrounded by chunks of asphalt. Roads are quickly being rebuilt and cut-off towns are now reconnected to the road system.

Yesterday I rode my bike out to a section of town still inaccessible by vehicle to check in on residents and document the rebuilding process for the town's Facebook page. I came across a utility worker leaning against his bucket truck as he paused for lunch. I knew I couldn't hug this burly, six-foot-plus man. So I shook his hand and looking straight into his eyes, said, "Thank you."

We chatted for a few minutes, saying we'd never seen anything like this and probably never will again.

"So where are you from?" I inquired. Utility crews from all over the country are here in Vermont to help restore power and communication, so I expected him to answer with some far-off state.

"Right up the road there," he pointed.

"Oh, we're neighbors," I said. "I'm Luke."

"I'm John. Good to meet ya." ✒

Luke Q. Stafford is a writer and business owner from South Newfane, Vermont. He lives with his wife, daughter and pooch in an old house on the Rock River, which now has beachfront property. This chapter is from his blog, a week after Irene.

3
Prattsville, New York

In just minutes, the whole town was gone, swept away as a flooded creek reached the rooftops.

By Michael Ryan

It was a strange pew to be sitting in on a summer Sunday morning. The floodwaters of Tropical Storm Irene were devouring downtown Prattsville, and John Young, stuck on his feed shed roof, was praying for strength.

He was shivering. It was raining insidiously. The only spot his brother, his father and mother, and he could find safe from the seething Schoharie Creek was a slippery metal roof.

Safe was a relative term.

Prattsville was getting the worst of it among its neighbors to the east and south who were contending with the Batavia Kill, the West Kill and the East Kill, all insanely over their banks. They combined forces with the Schoharie Creek outside Prattsville, and the Huntersfield Creek, which usually meandered through the heart of town, had changed into a raving lunatic.

Stella Cross, a Main Street resident, says she saw the country brook, blocked by a bridge, frothing in four directions before she evacuated, something she never dreamed would happen. It was real all right and nightmarish. It was nearing noon on August 28 and the Youngs, roof-bound with their three dogs, were thinking they might soon be meeting their maker.

Photo: Michael Ryan, courtesy of Hudson-Catskill Newspapers

It was raining, of course, when John Young (right) and his father Jim Young revisited the feed shed roof where they sat out the storm with mom Peggy Young and brother Brian Young. The trailer in the background replaces a building destroyed by the floodwaters.

"We weren't saying a lot," John Young remembers. Unlike a lot of folks, the Youngs, proprietors of the local Agway Store, had been preparing for the flood. They'd been down this road before—who in Prattsville hadn't?—and they'd spent the past few days elevating store goods and household possessions.

The height of the Schoharie Creek at 7:30 or so that morning was typical for a prolonged cloudburst. There was a certain comfort zone, recognizing familiar high-water marks. By 8:30, in a phenomenon experienced by everyone in Prattsville, the waters rose with brute flash force and almost inescapable speed.

It was disconcerting at first, then creepy, then ungodly. Whirlpools formed in their basement and the Youngs were forced to focus on areas that had never gotten wet in the past. Horses needed to be moved to a nearby pole barn. "It was weird. We usually couldn't get them into the stall without a fight, but they didn't resist," John Young said. "They were passive, like they knew we were trying to save them." The floodwaters kept surging and in what seemed like a few heartbeats, time became precious.

Trucks and cars floated in the Agway parking lot. Waves lapped up on the newly built greenhouse with its neat stone walls. The Youngs were as disoriented as the Huntersfield Creek.

"Everything was happening so fast," John Young said. "I was maneuvering cars out of the way, trudging between the store and the pole barn, and stuff was hitting me underneath the water. We started to feel like our lives were in jeopardy. We felt like we'd be okay in the store but then it started to move. We could hear beams cracking and popping."

The building was groaning and shifting on its century-old foundation. The shed roof with its wire mesh walls, roughly fifty feet away, was an unlikely last refuge.

Photo: Judith Grafe (FEMA)

A ruined house in Prattsville where Pam Young and her children survived the flood on the rooftop

"We knew the current was too strong. We couldn't get back if we went, but we had no choice," John Young said. "It was either that or have the store collapse on us. Merchandise we knew was on upper shelves was pouring out the door. This was already way beyond anything we ever imagined. We tied two garden hoses together for a rope and went."

Not quite one hundred yards away, at the submerged corner of Main Street and Washington Street, Prattsville town supervisor Kory O'Hara was watching the Youngs' life and death struggle with a sense of helplessness. The feeling would gnaw deeper as the day wore on, and it was being similarly felt in other peoples' hearts and souls in neighboring towns and villages.

O'Hara had gotten a cup of coffee at the Prattsville Diner shortly after dawn on Sunday and went to check his equipment

Photo: Michael Ryan, courtesy of Hudson-Catskill Newspapers

School buses from *Windham-Ashland-Jewett* floated away like toys in the bloated *Batavia Kill*, drifting more than a mile downstream.

Photos: Elissa Jun and Hans Pennink (FEMA)

Prattsville houses damaged by Irene.

repair station, on the north end of town. The Schoharie Creek, outside the back windows, was high but nothing out of the ordinary. O'Hara believed the community would be fine.

That would be the last time he saw his business intact. Twenty-four hours later, he offered a perspective, profound in its simplicity, on the horrific events that unfolded.

United States Congressman Chris Gibson was in town assessing the situation. O'Hara, giving a tour of the mayhem in a grungy ATV to Gibson, Greene County Legislature chairman Wayne Speenburgh and County Sheriff Greg Seeley, said, "We're used to floods around here.

"But this was no flood. I don't know what you call this thing." Many names would be uttered during the recovery that on the Saturday before the storm no one thought would be necessary. O'Hara had been alerted by Greene County Emergency Services director John Farrell on Saturday, that Prattsville was sited to receive a high volume of rain.

He relayed the information to local fire chief Tom Olson and

Photo: Hans Pennink (FEMA)

A Prattsville bathroom destroyed by Irene.

Photo: Michael Ryan, courtesy of Hudson-Catskill Newspapers
A message board tacked to a utility pole in the Great American Store parking lot in Prattsville was the most reliable means of communication in the days immediately following the deluge.

assistant chief Jim Dymond. "We didn't want to turn it into a scare. We went to a high alert for potential flooding," O'Hara says.

O'Hara and his brother Kipp had put the shop's tools up on Saturday night. After checking the station on Sunday morning they stopped by Young's Agway Store.

"Water was rising in the street a little bit but we drove over in a pickup truck," O'Hara said. "We could see what they were dealing with and said we'd come back to help. By the time we got back to the firehouse, the water was coming down Main Street like the Mississippi River. My brother went to get my grandmother who lives across from the station.

"When my grandmother got to the firehouse, there were about thirty elderly people inside, laughing, not thinking anything was different than a lot of other times," O'Hara said. "I swear, within minutes, water was gushing into the firehouse, first six inches and then eight and then a foot and more. Chief Olson

Photo: Michael Mancino (FEMA)

Dozens of volunteers participated in New York State's "Labor for your neighbor" campaign and lined up for buses in Prattsville that took them out to homes that awaiting cleanup from the flooding.

Photo: Judith Grafe (FEMA)

In the days after the storm, when the roads were blocked, ATVs were the best means of traveling from place to place.

started taking the people in an ambulance to the Hideaway Hotel, further up on Washington Street. The water got out of control," O'Hara said, snapping his fingers, 'like that.' We were afraid we'd lose the ambulance so we tied a chain to a backhoe. We got everybody out but Main Street was done. We were cut off from the firehouse," a stone's throw away.

Sometime between 10:30 and 11 a.m., amid a rush of 911 calls, "We were notified the Bakers were trapped and that trailers were starting to move," O'Hara said.

Steve Baker and his family own Moore's Mobile Home Park, across the street from O'Hara's repair station and within sight of the Route 23 bridge spanning the Schoharie Creek. O'Hara and a handful of volunteers made their way to the Bakers, cutting through drowning fields and backyards. The decision to evacuate the trailer park was made quickly.

Photo: Michael Ryan, courtesy of Hudson-Catskill Newspapers

An army helicopter hovers over a double-wide mobile home that was destroyed by fire at the height of the storm in Prattsville.

Photo: Michael Ryan, courtesy of Hudson-Catskill Newspapers

National Guard men and women were in the trenches, mucking out basements in Prattsville and surrounding towns, then returning to quarters after a long day. Here, in front of the Prattsville Diner, they carry buckets and other tools they used to clean out homes.

Photo: Michael Ryan, courtesy of Hudson-Catskill Newspapers

A street corner named disaster, at the entrance to Young's Agway Store in Prattsville.

"This was the most unbelievable scene ever," O'Hara said. "We had to invent a road through the fields, tearing down a stone wall to get through."

The water was monstrous. People were grabbing everything they could— kids, dogs, cats, parrots—and filling their cars. The rain was ridiculous. The mud in the fields was too deep to drive through. Volunteer fireman Mike Boerem had to pull the cars out one by one. Mothers and kids were screaming and crying.

"While we were doing all that, the fire siren went off," O'Hara said. "A few of us headed back toward the trailer park. We couldn't make it through. A brand new double-wide was burning slowly and as we were standing there a propane tank came skimming across the water, hit the trailer, and exploded. One of the firemen, Randy Brainard, got on his walkie-talkie and all he said was, 'It's a total loss. Heading back to quarters.' There was nothing more we could do but ride it out."

There would be no rest from the wickedness yet. Speenburgh telephoned to ask how it was going. "We told him it was bad. We needed helicopters," O'Hara said.

The water was remorselessly lifting and twisting houses. "We got word a guy was in his home, close to us," O'Hara said. "We made it to him using Mike Briggs's skidder. The guy was sitting in a chair in water up to his knees. He was yelling, 'I can't swim. I can't swim.' I've never seen a guy shaking like he was shaking."

Speenburgh called back to say the helicopters were a no-go. Seeley, though, was sending deputies and a rescue boat. The priority, when they arrived, would be getting Pam Young and her kids off the roof of her house, which was hauntingly tilted, near the trailer park.

Sixteen trailers got dislodged by the floodwaters and deposited with crushed cars and trucks in the road and woods along County Route 7, below the Route 23 bridge. Mary Lutz saw the ghostly caravan drift past her living room window from high ground. "I cried every minute," the 85-year-old Lutz said. It took workers two days to cut through the tangled mess.

Sheriff's deputies made their way to Prattsville, which was becoming increasingly isolated as bridges and roads collapsed throughout the county, and launched their rescue craft.

"John Young and his family were in a bind, but they'd have

Photo: Michael Ryan, courtesy of Hudson-Catskill Newspapers

A woman and two children wearing surgical masks to keep out the dust navigate Main Street in the early days of the recovery.

to wait," O'Hara said. "Pam Young [no relation] was in more serious trouble. Her 911 calls were heart-wrenching. The sheriff's boat went down Washington Street, made the right turn onto Main Street, lost control and capsized. The deputies had to cling to a porch at Beth's Cafe to save themselves. When they made it back to us, one of them said, 'I guess that wasn't a very good idea.' It seemed like it was at the time."

John Young and his family saw the sheriff's boat sink around noon or maybe four in the afternoon. Time had become irrelevant.

The gauges measuring the water flow in the Schoharie Creek were obliterated and the warning sirens had gone off at the Gilboa Dam, six miles north—not a good sign. Sirens sounding meant the dam, which is part of the New York City reservoir system, was threatened. As it turned out, the monitors broke at the dam too, causing the sirens to wail. The towns of Middleburgh and Schoharie, below the dam, were suffering hideous fates. John Young could sympathize but was in no position to help.

"Mostly what I remember doing is praying," said John Young, who on any other Sunday might have been kneeling, dry and devoted, in the Prattsville Methodist Church up the street. The church was more suited to Noah's Ark at the moment. "I was praying for strength, but for what, I didn't know," John Young said.

Photo: Michael Ryan, courtesy of Hudson-Catskill Newspapers

Rising above the rubble, the Dutch Reformed Church in Prattsville is slowly recovering.

"We could see black smoke from the fires burning and we heard an old barn breaking up behind us. Bulldozers, gasoline tankers and trees were going down the creek.

"Propane tanks snapped loose at the firehouse and were hissing. We thought the building would blow up. Why not? Everything we knew and understood had broken down."

Peggy and Jim Young, John's parents, were huddled together like soaked fawns. Months after the flood, Jim Young related a story about a group of New York City kids who were in town that day.

The kids and their guardians had seen the local Gun Club get sucked into the Schoharie Creek and started taking the house doors off their hinges to use as life rafts.

In the days and weeks after the floodwaters drained, Jim Young says he cried more than once as volunteers, perfect strangers, came to Prattsville to do whatever they could.

"I've seen the kindness of people so many times," Jim Young says. "They kept coming back and I would hug them and cry, and they'd come again and I kept hugging them and crying."

Nobody was doing much of anything on the shed roof except worrying about sliding off. The water was six feet deep inside the store, which was as fragile as a doll house.

Water was well over the Route 23 bridge, where the creek banks were compressed, where tons of debris had collected, and where O'Hara's repair station was trembling.

"My mom had her face buried in my dad's shoulders," John Young said. "The worst thing for me was trying to keep my mind stable. To keep my thoughts from straying too far. The creek sounded like a waterfall, constantly roaring." The concept was not far-fetched. Prattsville, at the storm's zenith, was pummeled with the 90-mile-per hour power of Niagara Falls.

"My brother Brian and I talked, like in a whisper, about—I can't believe I'm actually saying this—about what we would do if somebody floated past," John Young said. "We assumed it was going to happen. It was feeling like I was losing my grasp on things so Brian and I came up with a plan to save somebody. We'd been watching the debris going by, timing it. We figured we'd have twelve seconds. We decided if they were floating face down we couldn't do anything. If they were face up, we'd throw the garden hose to them. Hopefully they could grab it and wrap it around a tree further downstream."

Kory O'Hara was in the throes of the storm. People in town who had transported their cars to Washington Street before the flood had locked the doors.

"We couldn't move them," O'Hara said, adding to the mayhem. The men from the Melrose Fire Department, if they made it to town, would need all the space they could get.

There was only one sure way left into the flood zone, along hilly County Route 10, which became Washington Street when it reached Prattsville, running into Main Street.

Emergency personnel had to take numerous detours on remote rural back roads to weave their way in, so the men from Melrose were met like heroes when they arrived.

"They were like Navy Seals," O'Hara said. "They had Swift Boats and weren't messing around. They wanted to know who was in charge and who had to be rescued first. I told them Pam Young, so they set out down Washington Street, hanging onto the sides of their boat. They made the turn onto Main Street and the engine went dead. We didn't hear anything for a while. They finally radioed in that they had aborted the mission. They never made it past the Prattsville Tavern, only a few yards down the road.

"Their boat got caught in the current and wedged against a house. We decided to try a chain and rope rescue, going in the same way we'd gone to evacuate the trailer park. On the way, we found out that Anastasia Rikard was trapped in her house [a three-story, multicolored Victorian structure that would become an international symbol of Irene's destruction]. Rikard was unreachable until the waters waned as if by magic. "I thought the dam broke, they went down so fast," O'Hara said.

Pam Young and her kids were snatched from the roof by local resident Jeremy Marsh, and O'Hara got the relieving news that as far as anyone knew, no one had died. Things, however, went from bad to worse. "It was right about then I got a call from John Baker," O'Hara said. "He said my station was gone." More accurately, it was vaporized.

The Schoharie Creek dragged 86 years of O'Hara family history to a watery grave. The Youngs lost half their store and had damage to three homes.

Photo: Michael Ryan, courtesy of Hudson-Catskill Newspapers

Waiting to be relocated in Prattsville are Stephanie Braswell and her son Dylan, displaced by the seething Schoharie Creek which blasted a hole in the back of a business on Main Street.

It was painfully plain that O'Hara and the Youngs were not alone. Prattsville was buried in creek muck, fallen trees and cracked utility poles. Power would not be restored for weeks. State Route 23 was inaccessible and pocked with craters. The Route 23 bridge was scoured on both sides and teetering on the brink. Water mains were exposed six feet deep.

"A group of us walked from one end of town to the other," O'Hara recalls. "The town was empty. Main Street looked like a bomb went off."

O'Hara's initial journey through a very different downtown would not be the low point. Greater depths would be descended some days later. As a saturated Sabbath came to an end, the youngest town supervisor on the mountaintop crashed into a short and not very sweet sleep.

Monday the 29th of August was hot and sunny. O'Hara was back in the thick of it by 6 a.m., trying to absorb the hit and get a grip on the disfigurement.

Prattsville proper (2000 Census population: 665) had been

Photo: Michael Ryan, courtesy of Hudson-Catskill Newspapers

"God Save Prattsville" is painted on the home of Prattsville attorney Dave Rikard. The house became an internationally recognized symbol of the destruction. The condemned building has since been removed. The photo on the front cover of this book shows the house being demolished.

in existence more than 200 years. O'Hara's grandmother's house, built in 1785, predated official town founder, Colonel Zadock Pratt, namesake of the Pratt Museum and Pratt Rock, affectionately called the little Mount Rushmore. Pratt was a unique character. He served two terms in the US.Congress and while designing the town built a road distant from the Schoharie Creek, hoping to spare it from floods.

Levi Hill, a pioneer in the field of photography and the Smithsonian Institute-recognized father of color photos, is said to have used Prattsville as a backdrop for his historic first shots.

Ancestors of Prattsville's original settlers fought in the French and Indian War, and in 1825 Colonel Pratt developed the world's largest tannery in his town nestled in the Catskill Mountains.

A little too nestled on August 28, Prattsville never stood a chance as floodwaters surged down steep peaks and squeezed through narrow valleys, blasting into Main Street.

Nobody was ready for this storm. Grizzled volunteer firefighters who'd supposedly seen it all were as caught off guard as the next guy.

O'Hara, 35 years old, had been in office four years. His role as chief fiscal officer changed in the blink of an eye as the weight of the worst disaster in Prattsville's history was put on his shoulders.

Federal Emergency Management Agency consultants were air-lifted into town on Monday night. Gnarly, independent residents were already picking themselves up by their muddy bootstraps. Firefighters from the nearby town of Grand Gorge began cutting through the pile of mobile homes Monday morning and local farmer Carl Gockel showed up with his tractor, ready for duty.

O'Hara, by then, had his recovery team in place: his brother Kipp, John Young, town board members Jim Thorington and Bonnie Chase, BJ Murray, Charlie Gockel and Chief Olson. Carl Gockel literally plowed his way to the Great American Store parking lot in the center of town, and the recovery team set up base camp. The next move was anybody's guess.

There was no rule book or if there was it had been swept away with the local little league's game log which wound up at the Turtle Rock Cafe in Schoharie, a good thirty miles downstream.

"I'll be honest, a lot of it is a fog, thinking back," O'Hara says. "We were hacking through stuff you'd never believe if somebody had told you you'd be doing, the day before. I knew we needed lots of equipment in here." Speenburgh recruited John Halsted from the valley town of Coxsackie to bring a fleet of trucks.

"We were paralyzed, but he was able to restore the streets to passable by Tuesday morning," O'Hara said. "Clearing things out was one thing. The harder part was all the rumors."

More than 150 homes and businesses were impacted. Most of them were either condemned or listed as dangerous in the days following the flood. The facts were bad enough. Communications were sketchy. Rumors were rampant. They had to be checked out, just in case. It was exhausting, and meanwhile the town of Windham was facing its own grim reality.

The terrifying specter of the dams breaking had passed in Windham, but the town nine miles to the east of Prattsville was dealing with the death of Lorraine Osborn. Rumors spread on

Sunday, that the largest of the town's three flood-control dams had been breeched. "It sent shivers through me," Windham highway superintendent Thomas Hoyt said.

Hoyt also serves as contract officer for the Batavia Kill Watershed District, overseers of the dams. He had been advised that state police were knocking on doors, telling people five miles below the dam to get out. For anyone closer it was too late. Roads were already underwater. Nobody was going anywhere. The wall of water smashing through Big Hollow Valley to Windham would have brought immense loss of life.

Jay Fink, the station manager at Windham radio station WRIP, was on the air live at the time, giving hundreds of people their sole link to the outside world. When reports came in that the home of Bill Lonecke was getting bashed to pieces by the Batavia Kill out by the dam, Fink went briefly silent.

A seasoned pro, Fink won numerous awards for his work during Irene. He had no words for the dread. Ultimately, spillways on the dams were grotesquely eroded, needing major repairs, but the dams held.

Wheelchair-bound Lorraine Osborn was not so fortunate. Her mobile home was grabbed by the Batavia Kill shortly after her husband Bud had gone to an adjoining garage for a cell phone. The trailer got pinned in trees 75 yards downstream. "If you want to know the meaning of helpless, just ask Bud and me," said John Albert, a neighbor who tried in vain to reach her.

Some of Irene's most torrential rains, 16 inches in 12 hours, fell in the town of Windham, in the outlying hamlet of Maplecrest, where Mrs. Osborn was killed. The dams, built in the 1960s in response to Hurricane Donna, were designed to handle half that amount. People seeking answers for why the flood wreaked such havoc need search no further.

Windham endured its share of destruction. Main Street, in the shadow of Windham Mountain, an internationally known ski slope, was under six feet of water for several hours. Sidewalks were torn up. Sewer and water lines were damaged. Most homeowners and merchants had to slice out the bottom layer of sheetrock in their buildings, dehumidify the timbers and restore the walls, a common sight after Irene, as were the stacks of rubble in the streets.

Photo: Michael Ryan, courtesy of Hudson-Catskill Newspapers

Prattsville town supervisor Kory O'Hara indicates the high-water mark while contemplating the future from the Route 23 bridge. Floodwaters rose nearly 20 feet at the bridge, on the north side of town.

It was expected that most everything would be back to normal on Main Street by the end of 2012, small comfort to those residents in Maplecrest who lost their homes, and the Osborns.

As often happens amidst tragedy, there were instances of light-heartedness and irony. Scores of volunteers showed up in Windham to help muck out cellars neck deep in creek mud.

One group of muckers, bent on their task for hours, dug several feet without finding a floor. They approached the owner, wondering how far down bottom was.

"What do you mean? There's a crawl space but I don't have a basement," the woman said, congenially. "Well," the muckers said, "you do now."

Two women on the west end of Windham, two doors apart from each other, had never met prior to the flood but got to talking afterward, swapping stories. They discovered they'd both been displaced by Hurricane Katrina—one in the 9th Ward in New Orleans, the other in Biloxi, Mississippi—migrating to the mountains to stay dry.

Photo: Michael Ryan, courtesy of Hudson-Catskill Newspapers

Virtually every building in Prattsville was either condemned or listed as dangerous in the aftermath of Irene, including the home of Franz and Ilse Fuchs whose faces show the weariness shared by many Prattsvillians.

Water had never reached the sanctuary of the Lexington/ West Kill United Methodist Church in the town of Lexington along old Route 13A, until the Schoharie Creek sinned on flood Sunday.

Lexington, six miles southwest of Prattsville, had four key bridges blasted by Irene, including two on State Route 42 within a couple of miles of each other, spanning the West Kill. No guns were drawn, although there were rumors to that effect, when local residents patched one of the bridges that collapsed on one end.

A serious dispute ensued after Michael Pushman and his brother-in-law Brian Bloodgood took it upon themselves to fix the 120-foot span. They merely wanted to reconnect residents marooned on a newly created island between the two ruined overpasses, waiting four days for the waters to sufficiently drop.

Pushman and Bloodgood filled in around the creek and cobbled together a road. "It had a bit of a dip," Pushman said in an understatement, "but people could get through." Nobody minded going slowly, but as the project was nearing completion New York state transportation officials dropped by, saying they intended to rip the bridge out.

Their plan was to put in a temporary structure which would take at least two weeks, under ideal circumstances, removing the patched bridge in the interim.

A band of citizens took fierce exception. "We weren't going to let them tear it out and leave everyone stranded," Pushman said. The state insisted, saying the bridge didn't meet specs. That was obvious, but Pushman told the suits it was an extreme situation, a situation out of control in terms of normal, which was impossible to define anymore.

The head-butting lasted two days, causing the State Police to get involved. Common sense finally prevailed. The old span stayed. Lengthy extension ladders were propped up by Pushman on opposite sides of the gaping void created by the total collapse of the second bridge. Citizens parked vehicles on both sides, ascended and descended the rickety stairways, and went on their merry ways. Both bridges have since been replaced at a cost of $14.2 million.

Much less money would be welcomed at the Lexington/West Kill United Methodist Church, where the inner sanctum stayed unscathed through many floods since it was built in 1845. Nothing was sacred to Irene. A makeshift altar has been assembled in a second story dining hall for Sunday services, but something is missing even as something faithfully remains.

"It's sad, seeing what's happened," says church Board of Trustees treasurer Betty Hapeman, who went to mass there as a child, was married there, and had her children baptized there. Pews are scattered hither and thither and the altar railing has been set to one side. No one is sure when the church will be repaired, but "there is still a simple peace here," Hapeman said.

The town of Jewett, nine miles east and north of Lexington, similarly had roads and bridges wrecked, including the historic steel Miles Bridge, constructed in the late 1800s. Thomas Hitchcock, a former town councilman, has family roots as deeply entrenched as any mountaintop dweller, entwining two centuries. His father was a noted historian and onetime school superintendent, dating back to one-room schoolhouse days. If you weren't born a Hitchcock here, there's a good chance you married one.

Hitchcock hasn't budged far from where he spent his boyhood, cherishing the intimate connections. Irene "swallowed places where I used to play," Hitchcock said. "It took my breath away, how quickly it happened. My mother is 94 years old and my uncle is 92. They never saw anything like this in their lives."

Miles Bridge was annihilated by the East Kill five miles from where volunteer firefighter Don Muth and Jewett highway department crewman Waylon McCullar yanked a man from death's door.

Muth and McCullar were on the way to save a woman trapped in the second story of her home when they noticed a car off the road, wedged between trees. They were driving a backhoe since regular vehicles were of no use anymore, and they saw a man in the car with the East Kill swiftly surrounding his dog and him. Muth climbed in the backhoe bucket while McCullar lifted him toward the car window.

McCullar, seeing that Muth, with his firemen's turnout gear, couldn't fit through the window, leaped out of the backhoe, walked across the bucket and dove into the car.

"Waylon never thought about what he was doing until after he did it," Muth recalled. "All of a sudden he yelled to the guy, 'Hey buddy, your dog is friendly, ain't he?' You should have seen the expression on Waylon's face. Adrenaline can make you do amazing things."Muth freed the man but the dog, a Labrador retriever, panicked, swimming to the other side.

Weird things were going on in the town of Ashland too, on Route 23 halfway between Windham and Prattsville. The presence of the local quarry spared the tiny hamlet from serious harm. The floodplain widens as the Batavia Kill nears town, and while a few houses were badly damaged, on the Prattsville side, the spanking new municipal hall/firehouse went untouched.

Ashland had built a new facility after a fire in the winter of

Photo: Michael Ryan, courtesy of Hudson-Catskill Newspapers
No one died in this trailer in Prattsville but the disarray is evidence of the mindless wrath of Irene.

2010 razed the structure. The new place was used as a shelter during Irene. The roof didn't leak. Lula Anderson, a columnist for Ashland in the local weekly newspaper, the *Windham Journal*, had four feet of water in her house, but it stayed put. So did the track loader owned by town supervisor Richard Tompkins, although it took a while to prove it. The loader was in a twenty-acre, back field when Irene struck and absent the next day.

"We assumed, with the powerful current, it was somewhere between here and the Gilboa Dam," said Tompkins, who also runs RTE Transport, a trucking and excavation business.

All was forsaken following several fruitless searches until one of Tompkins' workers, Glenn Beechert, noticed a scrawny-looking white birch tree sticking out of the earth. It was exactly where the loader had been. It had no branches. "Glenn looked at it and said, 'That's kind of odd, don't you think?'" Tompkins recounts. "I said, 'Yeah, I guess so.'" Closer examination revealed it was no tree, but a cut piece of birch. Beechert started poking around and about a foot down hit something solid.

It was the top of the roll cage. "We thought maybe the cab had been torn off but we kept digging," Tompkins said.

Shovels flailed, dirt flew and, lo and behold the eight-foot tall loader was uncovered. The current had created a whirlpool, scouring the ground beneath, and lowering the machine like a sleeping baby.

"It was perfectly level, like the day we left it," Tompkins said, noting Beechert, a master with tools, restored the loader, returning it to the RTE Transport fleet.

Congressman Gibson was lucky to reach Prattsville on Monday, driving twenty miles to go five with so many roads and bridges out.

National Guard units were in the hills outside town, keeping out curiosity seekers, staying in the trenches on Main Street for weeks, mucking out cellars, kitchens and dens.

"This is a different world," one guardsman said. A sense of order, albeit amid incredible disorder, was enveloping Prattsville.

The calm was always balanced on a razor's edge, though, and closer to calamity ten days after Irene. It was raining buckets. New York Senator James Seward was in town as Hurricane Lee flooded Binghamton and the southern tier, heading for Prattsville. The Schoharie Creek was swelling.

O'Hara assigned young volunteer fireman Sam Rikard to keep a close eye on a stick of wainscoting salvaged from the debris and poked into the creek bank, measuring Lee's rise. An evacuation had been ordered earlier by the county, based on forecasts, but withdrawn by O'Hara. "The way I saw it, we were thirty minutes away from the death of our town," O'Hara said.

"I called the team in. We decided nobody leaves until we say they leave. We were the ones in harm's way, and we felt if we left too soon it would kill Prattsville."

Rikard called in every fifteen minutes. There were eleven lines scratched into the wainscoting. If the creek reached the tenth line, a mandatory evacuation would be undertaken. It got to nine before Lee mercifully swerved west. The cleanup kept rolling. September days repetitiously passed. Relief tents and Salvation Army meal vans lined Main Street.

Helicopters buzzed overhead. Main Street was transformed into a four-lane highway, packed with cars and trucks and

Photo: Michael Ryan, courtesy of Hudson-Catskill Newspapers

Brian Lowe, the head golf pro at Windham Country Club, would not have been able to stand up against the fury of the floodwaters of Tropical Storm Irene, which left behind massive piles of trees, woody debris and household possessions in streams, fields and streets.

muddied human beings stacked six to eight deep on ATVs, all with purpose.

The spirit of heavenly cooperation was cruelly disrupted by a 911 call regarding a young girl wedged under a trailer behind the Prattsville Diner. She'd been searching for her belongings.

"Things were going great. There were tons of heavy machines in town, people were digging out, and then that call came in," O'Hara said. "Things got chaotic in a hurry.

"The ambulance drove in, raising a dust bowl, and firemen were running, saying they had to have an excavator. They got the girl out, but just as they did another emergency call came in.

"Somebody had stopped breathing at the Prattsville Tavern. The ambulance was already out. The air was thick with dust. I thought everything was going to unravel.

"Then I got word the man died. That was rock bottom for me," O'Hara said. "I thought the stress and strain of the ordeal were settling in, and we were losing control of the town. "Then somebody said the man died in his sleep, a natural death. For some reason I can't explain, in that instant I knew what I had to do. I closed the street so the coroner could get through and do his work. The town went totally quiet."

A raindrop could have been heard falling. "All the machines stopped," O'Hara said. "We let the family get in there, move the body, and grieve."

Incomprehension still fills the eyes of many Prattsville residents as the recovery from Irene's destruction inches forward, infinitely more slowly than it occurred.

Acceptance is not easy. Most houses on the creek side of Main Street remain eerily lifeless. The east side isn't much better. Many houses have been torn down. Silt-ridden household possessions lay abandoned, untouched since the day of the flood, left askew as if suspended in time. "For Sale" signs dot the landscape.

Virtually every business has reopened to some degree, however, and the community is resolute that Irene will rue the day she demonically punished Main Street. The decision to rebuild was made by John Young even as he pondered his death. "There were moments when I was angry, sitting on the roof that day," Young says.

"When I saw all the work my dad and my granddad had put into the business getting washed away like it was nothing, and our homes getting destroyed, I'll admit I got angry. But one of the things I was praying for was an answer to the question, 'What do we do here?' I thought if the Lord wants us to rebuild, He's going to have to send people.

"We needed massive numbers of people to help us and I thought if they came it would be a miracle. Well, the miracle happened with the volume of people that came and are still coming. They are more powerful in their way than the flood. How many thousands of people for a town of 700 residents?

How can you sit there feeling blue and deny that many people?

"This may sound nuts," Young said, "but at this point, months later, it's tough for me to say I wish this didn't happen. Don't get me wrong. I don't mean to minimize that people are displaced.

"But it's beautiful to see prayers answered by what everybody's doing. If you didn't like somebody before the flood, that stuff was gone. Everybody was pitching in, all on the same page. There are so many ways this could have gone, and in the big picture, this can be seen as a beautiful experience. My family is tighter. We love each other more, in an understood way."

The boundaries separating properties and people disappeared in the aftermath of Irene. The same commonality will be required to pave Prattsville's future. The spring of 2012 showed up early in the mountains. Temperatures climbed into the 70s by mid-March following an unseasonably warm, practically snow-less winter.

Federal, state, New York City, county and local officials are dedicating considerable energy and funding to the

Photo: Michael Ryan, courtesy of Hudson-Catskill Newspapers

Wainscoting salvaged from the debris was used to measure water levels in the swollen Schoharie Creek as Hurricane Lee approached, 10 days after Irene struck.

Photo: Judith Graffe (FEMA)

This car in Windham got hit by it all . . .water, sand, and a trailer hitch.

rebuilding effort, led by Congressman Gibson, Senator Seward, Assemblyman Peter Lopez and New York State Governor Andrew Cuomo's Task Force Recovery Team.

Unprecedented productive gatherings of government bureaucrats and agency heads have taken place, and a group of Prattsville citizens captured the spotlight at a FEMA-sponsored National Disaster Framework Recovery (NDFR) forum in mid-March, in New York City.

Prattsville resident Annie Hull spoke on behalf of the community, advising forum attendees of three committees formed to create a new vision for the town, focusing on Housing, Economic Development and Community Enhancement.

It was clear that the tiny town Colonel Zadock Pratt built, inextricably bound to the Schoharie Creek, is providing inspiration for the NDFR's work. Prattsville is not forgotten.

Frustration is evident, though. O'Hara, seeking a third, two-year term, was defeated in the November 2011, elections by surprise write-in candidate and former supervisor Alan Huggins. Huggins resigned before taking office and O'Hara was returned to the post, for one year, by the town board, with uncertainty looming beyond the November 2012, vote.

Despite the hometown divisiveness, O'Hara has gained the respect of movers and shakers from the State Capital to Capitol Hill and says he is committed to seeing the recovery through.

"It largely depends on who tells the story as far as what the

Photo: Hans Pennink (FEMA)

Construction crews install new guard rails on Route 22 just outside of Prattsville.

legacy of this storm and my part in it might be," O'Hara said. "I don't have much time to think about it. Some people have no idea what we had to do just to get to the point where we could see the damage, much less fix it. The people in town who had true damage and the most need will tell the story properly."

Breaking down the cold hard numbers, O'Hara said, "It could cost anywhere between $25 million to $40 million to get things back to where they were on August 27.

"People in town were scraping by back then. I know the trouble we're in. I live here. I pay taxes here. I'm rebuilding my business here. We're developing a long-term vision for the town that may or may not work out, but I don't look at the town as in bad shape anymore. I see the small things we're accomplishing.

"I believe good can come from this, if we take advantage of the opportunities we're being given," O'Hara said. "I hope mine isn't the last generation to stick it out. I'm pretty sure of one thing. No matter how it all turns out, people will be talking about this thing for a long time."

With every certainty, the Schoharie Creek will trespass again.

How dangerous are floating propane tanks?

Many observers of the flash flood throughout the Irene Zone spoke with the authors of this book and frequently mentioned the white propane tanks of various sizes that floated down the streams. Dislodged from houses and mobile homes or even from large storage areas and carried downstream with the force of the water, they were often seen striking bridge decks and stream boulders. First responders often warned bystanders to keep away for fear of an explosion.

But just how dangerous were those tanks?

Not very, said a spokesman for the National Propane Gas Association.

"Tanks being tossed about in rushing water can be a hazard whether they have propane in them or not," said Bruce Swiecicki, senior technical advisor for the NPGA. "If there is propane in them, the tanks can be hazardous if they strike an object and suffer damage to the container or the valve. If that happens, propane may be released. Since propane is a flammable gas at certain concentrations of air, and if such a concentration exists and it finds a source of ignition, it could ignite."

But an explosion would be very unlikely, he said, because the containers were out in the open air. The valves on tanks attached to houses or trailers were probably left in the open position, although firemen in many areas went around and turned then off. Left open, the gas would eventually leak out, and the time it would take to do that would depend on how full they were, added Swiecicki.

Those who claimed that the floodwaters themselves smelled like propane were likely mistaken, Swiecicki said. "As long as the temperature is above -44°F, propane will vaporize, so I doubt there would be any mixing of water and propane." The more likely source of a propane odor, he said, was from a local land-based tank that was leaking.

Bland white propane tanks from the Irene Zone made a long journey downstream, but most of them looked identical. The two tanks located at the Whetstone Studio for the Arts in Brattleboro were the exceptions. A local artist had painted a pastel scene featuring a Hobbit and flowers on them.

"They were the most beautiful tanks in America," said gallery owner David B. Parker.

They floated away downstream like the others, but because of their distinctive markings, observers noted them floating down the Connecticut River. The last reported sighting of the tanks was in Windsor Locks, Connecticut, over fifty miles away.

"My daughter in Florida was watching CNN and saw them there," said Parker. "She called me up to tell me the tanks were on television."

4
Wilmington, Vermont

Viewing their town's destruction from the top of Ray Hill, residents watched an artist's studio float away.

Residents of many towns caught by Irene's rampage complained later that they didn't have enough warning to prepare for the flash flooding that was about to engulf them, but the town of Wilmington had been warned for decades by a sign right in the middle of town.

There, at the intersection of routes 9 and 100, on the side of the two-story clapboard building that houses the town's police department, a wiggly painted line showed just how high the water had risen in the Deerfield River during the hurricane of 1938. It was about five feet above the sidewalk, on the other side of Main Street from the river, and it seemed to most of the residents who passed it every day little more than a historical marker, a bit of folklore or ancient history.

"I think no one actually thought it would happen again," said Lisa Sullivan of the Mount Snow Chamber of Commerce and owner of Bartleby's Books. "Most people weren't even alive in 1938."

Today there is a second line painted on that wall, not quite a foot higher than the previous one, marking the level of the river's rise from Tropical Storm Irene.

In the early morning of August 28, residents gathered at Dot's

61

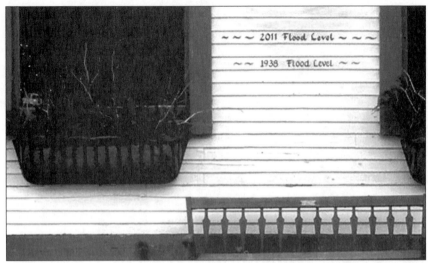

Photo: Craig Brandon

The flood levels from the 1938 and 2011 hurricanes are recorded on the wall of the police station in Wilmington, Vermont just to the right of this window. The bottom line is for the 1938 hurricane and the upper one is for Irene. The Deerfield River is to the left of this photo, across the street and down into a twelve-foot ravine.

Photo: Ann Manwaring

The flooded Deerfield River overflowing its banks in Wilmington.

Photo: Ann Manwaring

The river flows over the Main Street Bridge from the right, in front of Dot's Restaurant, and flows down West Main Street. This was taken before the river reached its highest level.

Restaurant, right in the center of town, just a few dozen yards from the 1938 sign, just like any other morning. The weather was a major topic. Some said they thought Vermont had "dodged the bullet," because Hurricane Irene, which weather maps showed had been pointed right at them, had dissipated and wind speeds had decreased. Others debated the local pastors' decisions to cancel church services that morning, which seemed to many to have been premature.

Meanwhile, the rain continued to fall in torrents, and high above the quaint little tourist town, in the mountains where the ski slopes of Mount Snow and Stratton provided the attraction that drew the winter tourists, a giant tidal wave of water seven feet high had formed in the Deerfield River. Many of the shops had not yet opened and their owners were unaware of what was about to happen.

Survivors credit the town fire chief, Ken March, with going shop to shop and house to house on Sunday morning like Paul Revere, spreading the warning that the water was coming. He closed the Main Street bridge over the river and made sure that Selectboard Members Jim Burke and Susie Haughtwort were

Photo: Ann Manwaring

Debris, including trees and parts of buildings, flowed over the bridge with Dot's Restaurant in the background. On Ray Hill, behind Dot's, Wilmington residents watched the destruction unfold.

ready to remove the irreplaceable town records, the ones that recorded who owned what in the town. They saved about 75 percent of them before the offices were flooded, often performing a kind of triage as they tried to determine which to save and which to let go as the water level rose in town hall.

Then March had to rescue his own firehouse, removing the equipment to higher ground before it was washed away in the flood. They rescued the trucks, but the office, the meeting and training room, and tens of thousands of dollars worth of equipment were ruined.

While most of the businesses had not yet opened, Sullivan was in her bookstore with her husband at 8:30 debating whether the rising river, which normally flowed behind the shops on the other side of the street, was going to be a problem.

"We got breakfast sandwiches from Dot's and there was no water in the streets then, but later we could see that the back

Photo: John Redd

While engineers check on the condition of the Main Street bridge on Sunday evening, residents get their first look at the damage.

parking lot across the street was flooded, and we could see down on the west end of town some water coming in, and we could see water coming over the bridge." An hour later there was a foot of water in the store. "We decided we needed to do some things. We brought the computers upstairs and we ran around the store taking books from the bottom shelves and putting them on the top shelves."

With Main Street flooding, their doors were holding back a significant amount of the water so they had to make a decision.

"My husband was concerned about the building. He thought there was too much pressure and we would lose the whole front of it. So we opened the door and let the water in and we started to smell propane and that's when we ran for it." They ran up the hill behind the store to Rayhill Road, high above the town,

Photo: John Redd

On Monday, building inspectors, including architect Joseph Cincotta, right, examine the damage inflicted on Main Street by Irene.

where residents had gathered in amazed groups, watching as Irene tore their town apart.

"It was like being in a Stephen Spielberg movie," said Joseph Cincotta, an architect who witnessed the devastation from the hillside."It was so surreal. I'm here and I'm watching this, but I have nothing to compare it with. I am watching nature at a scale and level I have not seen before. I was looking at it and listening to it and experiencing it, but I wasn't accepting it."

Meg Streeter, real estate agent and town selectman, was also on that hill, unable to get to her office, which was on the other side of the Main Street flood.

"On the way there I started to see how much water was gushing out of everywhere," she said. "Every tree, every piece of grass.

Photo: John Redd

Beth Leggiere's Yarn Shop on Monday after the flood. While knitted garments remained on the walls, the furniture and yarn skeins were gone and the carpets pulled up.

By the time I got to Route 100 it was a river." She stood there on the hill with the others and watched as Dot's Restaurant became an island in the river, flooded on both sides by the raging water, which was flowing in chocolate brown waves down the middle of the street. The Deerfield's normal course is to flow under the

Photo: Ann Manwaring

Skeins of yarn from Beth Leggiere's shop litter Main Street.

Main Street bridge next to Dot's and then make a sharp right turn behind West Main Street. Now the water was flowing over the bridge and making the right turn right through the middle of town. "All these logs and trees and propane tanks and parts of houses were just floating down. It was really frightening."

Also perched on Ray Hill was Beth Leggiere, whose yarn store, HandKnits, was clearly visible across the flood on North Main Street, next to the Maple Leaf Brew Pub.

"It looked to me like the windows were still in and the air conditioner was still in the window so I was sort of being overly optimistic," said Leggiere. "I thought everything would still be there." It would take another twenty-four hours before her optimism would be crushed.

The most dramatic moment of the flood came when the two-story yellow building that housed Ann Coleman's recently renovated studio on West Main was picked up in a single piece, including its concrete slab foundation, and pushed down the street. In a few seconds it crashed into a telephone pole and broke into pieces. The slab plunked down in the middle of the street while pieces of the building floated down the river into the Harriman Reservoir. Coleman wasn't there to watch the event live but has since posted the YouTube video of it on her website.

The plate glass windows in the front of the Maple Leaf Brew Pub on North Main broke, and the tables and chairs were pulled out into the stream and floated off through town, joining the tree trunks, appliances, lumber, furniture and lawn furniture that

Photo: John Redd

The Wilmington Chamber of Commerce building on Monday.

Photo: Lisa Sullivan

A National Guard soldier stands by as a front loader gathers thousands of water-damaged books for the landfill.

were rushing down the river, which was now in the center of town.

Meg Streeter, who could watch her office being flooded from Ray Hill, called the woman who lived upstairs and asked her to go down and rescue what she could from her office.

"She ran down the stairs and retrieved my computer tower and my real estate files. She stayed in that building during the entire flood. There was no way for her to get out. She was extremely lucky that the building stayed there. We were lucky there wasn't an explosion from all those propane tanks floating down. I'd say that was the most frightening thing."

While most residents were content to watch the flood from a distance and try to make sense out of what was happening, others became disoriented. A woman driving a minivan north on South Main Street toward the closed bridge became immobilized in the water and stayed there, unable to get out, with the water flowing all around her.

"Our town road foreman, Bill Hunt, had to get a back loader and go rescue her," said Streeter.

Ivana Taseva, 20, a native of Macedonia who was working at Mount Snow, was driving a car on Route 100 north of Wilmington when it was caught in the current. Two passengers in the car were able to get out safely, but Taseva was caught in the river and pulled underwater. Her body was found near the Deerfield Valley Elementary School. She was the only Wilmington fatality, but there were other near misses. A misguided man in a kayak attempted to paddle down Main Street and was pulled under when his boat tipped over. Observers thought he had drowned but he emerged from the water near Church Street.

Lisa Sullivan watched a bookcase float by that still had someone's wedding photo on one of the shelves.

By 3 p.m. the water began to subside, and by 6 p.m. the Deerfield was back within its banks and the true extent of the damage became clear. The town center was full of mud and pieces of buildings. Nearly every building in the main part of town had been damaged. The pavement was torn up and scattered; the town was entirely cut off from the outside world because large sections of Routes 9 and 100 had been washed away. The only route into town was through North Adams on Massachusetts Route 8 to the south, and it was on that route that the National Guard arrived the next day. With the Main Street bridge closed until engineers could certify that it was safe and most of the town blocked off by police and soldiers to prevent looting and injuries from collapsing buildings, it took some time for residents and shop owners to understand the full extent of the damage. But the news leaked out via videos that had been posted on YouTube. It was bad. Very bad. The quaint little village street that attracted so many tourists crossing Vermont now looked like it had suffered a terrorist attack.

"No one was thinking that we would get four feet of water right in the middle of Main Street," said Sullivan, the book store owner. "We got clearance from the National Guard to come in and take a look for an hour. The shelves were knocked over and there were books and mud splayed all over the place." Nearly her entire stock of books, some 17,000 of them, were ruined and could not be saved. They had to be loaded onto a payloader and taken to the landfill.

"Those first couple of days everything seemed so surreal

Photo: Craig Brandon

Painter Ann Coleman holding a print of a painting she made of Wilmington in better days. The print was washed away in the flood and later rescued.

that I don't think I was processing anything," said Sullivan. "There's a certain amount of disconnectedness because it is so unbelievable." Unable to even think about all the work it would take to restore her business, she put on her other hat, as head of the chamber of commerce, and went to work helping other businesses that had been destroyed. She talked with the press and state and local officials about funding and insurance. "There were lots of little meetings all day long," she said.

Beth Leggiere had received a phone call Sunday night warning her that the front window of her yarn shop had been broken and water had flowed through it, taking everything with it.

"I knew it was going to be bad, but I assumed there would be something left to salvage," she said. "Then I got another call, telling me it was very, very bad. It wasn't until Monday morning that I drove down and finally saw it. The entire store, everything inside it, was gone. All of my shelving was gone. I had a big IKEA chest, very heavy, but it was gone, washed down into the lake. The whole room was empty, like I had never moved in there."

The skeins of yarn that had been on those shelves had washed down the river, but portions of them had become caught on signs, fences and buildings; it hung everywhere, discolored and torn, like rainbow spider webs hanging from buildings, signs and lampposts.

As she described in December what happened three months earlier, Leggiere was still visibly shaken and found it difficult to speak. She still has problems when it rains, she said, but the "water dreams" that haunted her in the first week are not so much a problem anymore. She is sure about one thing. She is never going to own a shop in Wilmington again. She and her husband are looking at purchasing a small shop in Brattleboro, well above the floodplain.

"At first I had trouble with hard rains, and I am still probably eating more than I should," she said. "There are a lot of things to have nightmares about, but I wouldn't call them nightmares. I'm not waking up screaming or sweating or anything. There are other, more important things in life."

Andrea Berg, owner of a gift shop called Picknell's Barn, was able to rescue two bags full of stuffed animals and wine from her shop, but the Main Street building was destroyed. She told an interviewer that business had been up 28 percent in 2011 before the storm hit. Now she was out of business.

Also still shaken from her August 28 experience was Ann Coleman, the artist whose entire Main Street studio had been lifted up and carried away in the flood. She had recently completed the renovation of the studio from "an ugly, smelly wreck of a place" into an architecturally designed state-of-the-art studio, a $400,000 investment. "We were nearly done. All we had to do was put in a handicapped ramp, and the plumber had just finished the bathroom. Two days before my husband put on the first coat of yellow paint. The guy from the window treatment place was putting the UV protection on the windows to protect the artwork."

On Friday, her husband, listening to the news about the

Photo: Ann Manwaring

Senator Bernie Sanders, center, comforts Al Wurzburger, owner of the 1836 Country Store in Wilmington, outside the store in the week after Irene.

approach of Irene, suggested removing the artwork from the gallery. "I poo-pooed the idea. We were used to flooding in Wilmington, but I was thinking about wind and not rain." On Sunday, hearing reports about Wilmington from friends and watching YouTube videos of the river rushing through town, they attempted to get into town but gave up when all the roads were blocked. "We should probably go home while we still can," she had said.

At about 4 p.m. people who had been into town began telling her that her entire building was gone, that it was not there any more, that it had floated away, but she refused to believe it. When she got to the roadblock in Main Street and told the policeman who she was, she was warned that it was very bad. When she was allowed to go down and take a photo, she was asked to prepare herself again. It was going to be bad.

"So I looked down the street where the studio used to be, and I could see there was nothing there. I called my mom and told her. People were all around me telling me they were sorry for me, and it still didn't really sink in that everything was gone. We had it exactly the way we wanted. It was perfect, just what we wanted, and people told us it was the best building in town and now it's gone."

In addition to the building, Coleman lost 38 original paintings,representing several years worth of work, and 400 prints, half of which were framed—all of them washed down the river into the Harriman Reservoir. In the weeks after, people began finding pieces of her building and returning them to her at her home. One of her signs was retrieved, and someone found an armoire from her shop on the shore of a lake downstream. A pastel painting that had been exhibited in Boston and New York turned up in the reservoir, but the center of the painting had been washed away, leaving only the edges.

"I think it's amazing that it is in as good a shape as it is," she said. "That water was really nasty, really toxic. But I suppose it could be redone." Other artists in town have exhibited paintings inspired by the flood, including her friend, Jim McGrath, who painted a flood scene called "From my Window," but Coleman said she didn't think she would do that. "That's not my style," she said. "My stuff is more focused on joyful things."

The YouTube video of her studio floating down the river is on her website and she can manage to watch it now, but she is still hesitant to talk about that day. She is already working with her architect to build a new building on the same site and she is painting again, after a year spent renovating the building and grieving for its loss.

"I get bummed about how much work is ahead. I was so looking forward to being done with this project because I had a lot of sleepless nights and a lot of all-nighters."

Brian McIntryre and his family had to spend several days in shelters after their home at 10 Church Street was severely damaged when water entered it on Sunday. His seven-year-old daughter woke the family to tell them that they had to leave. The water was climbing up the side of their cars in the driveway by the time they left.

With so many bridges and highways blocked or eroded away, the National Guard had to bring in a water tanker, military style Meals Ready to Eat and fuel for Wilmington's 1,876 residents. The Guard set up camp at the intersection of Route 9 and Route

100 South, in a flat section of land that was usually home to a flea market. Until the Main Street bridge was determined to be safe, one side of town was cut off from the other. The damaged buildings and the National Guard Humvees running through town made it look more like a war zone than the quaint New England town it had been just a day before. The skies hummed with helicopters bringing in television news crews and politicians. Vermont Senators Patrick Leahy and Bernie Sanders and Gov. Peter Shumlin arrived wearing surgical face masks to protect them from the toxic dust that blew in clouds down the middle of Main Street.

Meanwhile, structural engineers and architects like Joe Cincotta were going door to door downtown, assessing the damage, looking at structural damage and placing red tape across the doors of buildings that were too dangerous to enter.

"Our historic downtown was just destroyed," he said. "I was going into absolute chaos. It was like walking onto a movie set. I could not believe this was my town I was looking at. They look like the buildings I knew, but they were just eviscerated. The windows were gone. The insides were washed away, and everything was replaced by this beautiful, velvet layer of silt, sparking under the bright unforgiving sunshine. You were squinting in the sunlight. It was such a contrast. It seemed wrong. We should be looking at this under a soft cloudy sky."

Some of the buildings were condemned and others had been pushed so far off their foundations that they required heavy equipment to set them upright again. Dot's Restaurant, the unofficial center of the community, where everyone met for coffee, had been right in the eye of the storm, its back wall bashed in by water running on both sides and through the center of the building. Its neon sign was the town's unofficial landmark. On Monday it was a mess of peeling siding, broken windows and hanging boards. Although the 1832 building was found to be structurally sound, there was still some question about what would happen to it, since it had been a restaurant for 111 years. John Reagan, the owner for thirty years, found it difficult to talk on the telephone about the future of Dot's, but vowed that it would be rebuilt, though probably not exactly as it had been before. It might become a seasonal business, he said. Although its foundation was found to be sound, nearly all of the structure would have to be replaced.

"People were just walking through town and were blown away by what they were seeing," said the Reverend Emily Heath of the Wilmington Congregational Church. "Everyone had the same look on their faces. They were in shock. It was like a war zone. Whole pieces of pavement had been pulled up and pushed aside. Stores and restaurants we had visited for years had their windows blown out. The physical devastation was beyond what you could imagine until you actually saw it."

People in the surrounding valleys who had lost their homes or could not get home because the streets and bridges were gone had to spend the next few nights sleeping in cots in the Twin Valley High School, where hot meals were available for those without electricity.

Bartleby's Books opened on Black Friday, the day after Thanksgiving, and the store was mobbed with customers who stood in a long line to get inside. With her bookshelves destroyed in the flood, Sullivan was able to buy shelves from her former competitors, the Borders Bookstores that had just closed stores in Keene, New Hampshire and Metheun, Massachusetts.

Construction was still going on at the Maple Leaf Brew Pub. Lori Downing, owner of the Bean Head's coffee shop, which lost its coffee grinders, cappuccino maker, refrigerator, freezer, panini grills, meats, cream cheeses and coffee during the flood was hoping to open in time to serve the skiers visiting Mount Snow, but at least a dozen business owners have thrown in the towel and won't be back. For them, the national recession in addition to Irene meant it was just not worth the frustration any more.

Reverend Heath said she spent a lot of her time in the next few weeks comforting parishioners about their losses. "They kept asking me why God was punishing us," she said. "My take was that after this horrendous thing we were going to see God's hand in the recovery. God can help turn a bad thing into a good thing." Besides the physical loss, she said, people were dealing with emotional and psychological problems. "I don't think anyone sprung right back. People became functional and operated on autopilot, but there had been a death in town.

Photos: Craig Brandon

Steve and Susan Wright of Woodford, Vermont, hold a photo of the famous "Stone House" that Steve built between Route 9 and Roaring Brook. Below is all that remains of the house after Irene battered it with water and boulders.

People were doing everything they could to get back to normal, but nothing was normal. It was a whole new ball game. I saw a lot of people who just needed someone to talk with. A lot of them were dealing with depression and some were struggling with trauma responses, anxiety, post-traumatic stress disorder." Staying busy helping each other worked, and working at 200 percent all the time was a king of therapy," she said. "But then we reached this second stage where we had to really deal with the reality—that is going to take a lot of time."

"I was wearing two hats because I was president of the chamber of commerce so I was spending a lot of time thinking about what was going to happen to our town, helping other people in town, dealing with the media and government officials," said Sullivan. "We had all kinds of little meetings. I was on the phone from the time I woke up until I went to bed at night. In some ways the bookstore was the easiest piece of the problem because it was very straightforward. First we need to get the mud out, then we need to fix the building; we need to buy shelves and we have to order more books. That seemed so much easier than helping people deal with insurance companies and government regulations."

While most of the local business owners are rebuilding, Sullivan says she understands why some are not.

"These people have dedicated many years of their lives to something and when they see all of that destroyed it takes a toll emotionally," she said. "Dot's is the heart of the town, the one business that everyone would rally around, not just residents but tourists too, and that puts a lot of pressure on the Reagans. It made it through the 1938 flood and it's adored by everybody. Everyone asked about it. It's a big part of the community."

"Everybody has gone through stages," said Streeter. "The emergency work helped people recover from the initial shock and a lot of these people are used to working really hard, but as time wears on you see more and more people who are really depressed. People think that they are fine, that they survived the worst, but then they remember all the important things they lost. Lately people have realized that we are not only coming back, but that things will actually be better. It's a chance to make improvements and Bartleby's Books is a good example of that."

Photo: Craig Brandon

As recovery work continued in Wilmington in the months after Irene, this sign cropped up everywhere, helping residents keep up their courage.

On day two when people were throwing all the ruined stuff out into the street, Lisa Sullivan went around asking people how they were doing. She was very inspirational. Not everyone could cope during those first few days."

When the mud dried and turned into dust, everyone wore surgical masks to protect themselves from the toxic dust, and the huge waves of flies that arrived, feeding on the mounds of debris that had been tossed out into the street. Eventually the town supplied dumpsters to deal with what had become a safety hazzard.

The recovery process produced some extraordinary discoveries as well. At the Wilmington Baptist Church, the upstairs sanctuary was spared but the fellowship hall in the basement was engulfed nearly up to the rafters.

"We tried to go down there on Monday but we were turned back by the National Guard," said Pastor Doug LaPlante. "On Tuesday we had to make our way through the mud and debris.

Everything was floating and the refrigerators had been turned upside down, one on top of the other. There was a steel chair on top of a four-drawer file cabinet. We had volunteers who showed up from as far away as Florida, people who weren't afraid of two inches of mud."

Workers tore out the ruined sheetrock on the walls in the basement; it was a lot of work and people were very discouraged," he said. Layer after layer of ruined walls were exposed until they came to a plaster wall that had a pastoral forest scene painted on it. When he examined this wall carefully, LaPlante said it was clear that it had been part of a mural from an earlier history of the church. He could see a water line on the mural that had to have come from the previous hurricane in 1938.

"It had been there for 72 years," he said, "waiting for us to find it." But when he tried to cut it out to save it, the mural fell into pieces. Luckily he had taken a photo of it. "It was a tremendous message to us that God had blessed us once and he will do it again. That life will go on."

The discovery of the mural led him to look at the church's records from the previous flood, and he found a poem that had been composed by one of the members of the congregation:

When last year there came the flood
Which seemed too much for flesh and blood,
Our pastor worked with might and main
To make things seem all right again,
Piano gone and books galore,
And many things that are no more,
But no discouraged sigh was heard
But the faith of God's own word
That all things together work for good
To those who love him as they should.

"It was deja vu," said Plante. "The same thing happened back then. Everything was ruined. All we saved this time were the dishes and the communion set. It's a story of hope. With God all things are possible. People lost their homes, lost their businesses, but then we had all of these people helping each other. The community has come together remarkably. There's a lot of good

Photo: Wendell Davis (FEMA)

FEMA's Danny Baker talks with Maple Leaf Malt Brewery Company owner, Margaret Ziolkowski, about the damage Tropical Storm Irene caused to her business in Wilmington.

that has come out of this." The church recovered enough to open again on December 23 for the beginning of Christmas services.

By year's end a lot of the damage had been repaired, and Christmas lights and decorations were on nearly every building in town, even the ones that were still empty, but residents were still feeling the impact. At the end of September, to mark a month of recovery efforts, the town held a concert called "Floodstock," organized by Christophe Jalbert, owner of the Apres Vous

Restaurant and Bar. For hundreds of people it was their first break from the long days and expensive recovery. Many of them said they were still not sleeping normally, especially when it rained, bringing back memories of August 28. But there were good memories as well, especially of the hundreds of volunteers who showed up from as far away as Philadelphia and Maine to help with the recovery, enough to make even tough veterans like Al Wurzburger, owner of the 1836 Country Store, shed a few tears. "I couldn't help it," he told an interviewer. "No one is trained to deal with the total destruction of a town."

Towns near Wilmington were also extensively damaged, including the Jacksonville section of Whitingham, where chunks of Routes 100 and 112 were washed away. State Trooper Eric Hawley, who lived on Gates Pond Road across from the Jacksonville General Store, was not home when the brook behind his house rose up to engulf his living room. He was out on patrol helping others deal with the flood. Irreplaceable items

Photo: Wendell Davis (FEMA)

Michael Harris, FEMA mitigation team member, shows the high water mark on the Norton House. Tropical Storm Irene raised the water level of the Deerfield River 28 feet above normal.

like family pictures, yearbooks and framed photos had to be laid out on a tarp to dry before being placed in a storage trailer. His girlfriend, Lisa Gardner, had to be rescued from the house after the stream tore away its foundation.

Brett Morrison, who lived on Ball Mountain Road in Jamaica, watched as the flooded Ball Mountain Brook tore away the foundation of his house and carried it down the stream, which had turned into "a savage beast," as he put it. "It looked like liquid earth." No one was hurt, but on Monday, all that remained of his house was the back porch. A temporary access road ran through where his kitchen and family room used to be. Witnesses said four houses from Ball Mountain Road smashed into the Depot Street Bridge and exploded into pieces upon impact.

After the flood, Morrison worked with a class from Burr Burton Academy to clean up other residents' properties; he found pieces of his home embedded in the dirt, including a wadded up mass of metal that had once been his kitchen stove. A pink blob, he said, used to be his daughter's body pillow.

In Wardsboro, every road out of town was washed out by 3 p.m. on Sunday, and four houses were destroyed by flooded streams and rivers, including the Wardsboro Brook. Others were perched so precariously over the flooded streambeds that residents were forbidden to enter until they could be shored up.

About twenty miles to the west of Wilmington, the town of Woodford dealt with a Route 9 bridge collapse over Roaring Brook that closed the highway and cut the water supply to Bennington. It also removed a landmark that had a special significance for Steve Wright, one of the Woodford selectmen.

The house, called the Stone House when it was featured in various Vermont magazines, had been built by hand by Wright, who hauled 150-pound, watermelon-shaped stream stones one by one to the house's location on Route 9 near the town hall, beginning in 1978. Each evening he would haul about 350 stones and set them up with mortar the next day.

"People told me it couldn't be done, that you couldn't build a house that way, even my Dad told me that," he said. But he had promised his wife Susan that he would build her a big house and that was the only way he could afford it.

"Every one of those rocks came out of Roaring Brook. Every

Photo: Craig Brandon

Come spring, the owners of Dot's announced they would rebuild.

day I would go out and get those stones," he said. But he wasn't looking for just any stones. He selected the ones he wanted for size and color, and then mortared them into place, starting with the garage on the east side and then moving west to the sunken living room, the fireplace and the bedrooms. The project took seven years and wasn't completed until 1984.

"We lived in a trailer while it was being built," he said. "No one could see what we were doing from the road until we moved the trailer. Then people stopped on the highway all the time, taking pictures of it. We almost had a couple of accidents out there because people were stopping all the time on the highway."

On August 28, 2011, Wright was on a hunting trip in Colorado. It wasn't until he got back to civilization that he began to get calls from Vermont. "When I heard that there was water I wasn't concerned at all," he said. "The house was designed to take water." Even when his brother told him "the Stone House is gone," he refused to believe it. "There's just no way that house could be gone." But everyone in town was sending him photos, and when he finally arrived back in Woodford a week later he saw the damage for himself.

Since the wood frame houses on either side of his house suffered only minor damage, Wright said Roaring Brook seemed to have targeted his house. It wasn't just the water, but car-sized boulders rolling down the hill that deflected off the far shore and came at his house at an angle with the power of a battering ram. "The house was strong enough to sustain that for a long time, but neighbors said they saw boulders striking it relentlessly."

For days, town residents drove by with tears in their eyes, feeling the loss with Steve and Susan of the unusual and remarkable house. Wright, who has no plans to rebuild, said he understood the strange and mystical notion that the Roaring Brook had somehow targeted his house so it could reclaim the stones that Wright had taken.

"I have never found a single one of those stones," he said. They were either washed away or were buried under yards of silt and rocks that make up the stream's new bed."

On March 19 the recovering business district of Wilmington got its best news of all. Dot's Restaurant, the landmark community

Photo: Ann Manwaring

A National Guard Humvee on North Main Street.

center and iconic eatery that had stood damaged in the center of town for six months, announced that it would stay in business at the intersection of Route 9 and Route 100.

In a ceremony in which Goveror Peter Shumlin joined, John Reagan, the owner of the restaurant since the 1980s, said the building, which had taken a direct hit from the Deerfield River, was thought at first to be too damaged to be repaired. A second opinion from a structural engineer, however, showed otherwise and a plan was forged.

Exactly when it opens depends on how soon they raise the money. They set up a website at rebuilddots.com to collect donations. "We got lots of help from the community and it's going to take a lot of help," said Patty Reagan, John's wife. "We can't do it on our own."

"There is no better example of community spirit, of tenacity, of caring about each other, and of pulling ourselves up by our bootstraps than what you see right here at Dot's," Shumlin said.

᠙

Photo: White River National Fish Hatchery

White River National Fish Hatchery damaged in Bethel, Vermont.

Hatchery damaged: Managers fear "rock snot"

O f all the buildings that were damaged by Irene, one would think that a fish hatchery would be immune. After all, how much damage could a little bit of water do in a place like that?

It turns out there was plenty of damage at the White River National Fish Hatchery in Bethel, Vermont, where the tanks that hold the fish were covered by as much as eight feet of mud. Just before the flood, the tents that surround the tanks were zipped up around them to protect the fish as much as possible.

"A lot of the fish went right to the bottom of the pools to protect themselves," said Ken Gillette, project leader at the hatchery. After the flood, when volunteers helped remove the mud from the tanks, they found a lot of dead fish, of course, but about 60 percent were still alive.

"The water was pretty muddy," he said, "but we were surprised to see how many were still alive." The older and larger fish survived Irene's abuse much better than the smaller ones, which succumbed in large numbers.

The hatchery buildings sustained severe damage, including twisted metal on the fish tanks and six-inch concrete floors that were dug up, broken and shifted. Work has already begun to rebuild the facilities, but a lingering concern was contamination from "rock snot," an invasive algae that lived in the White River, but might have contaminated the pools of fish destined for places where the algae had not yet contaminated the water.

Some 3,000 salmon that were in the hatchery on August 28, some as large as five pounds, were supposed to be used to stock lakes in Western Massachusetts for a winter ice fishing program. Although it was not known if the fish had been contaminated, the fish were still fit for human consumption. So, because of the potential of spreading the algae, the fish, which were considered perfectly safe for human consumption, were donated to Native American tribes throughout the Eastern United States to be used as part of tribal ceremonies.

Another 3,400 smaller salmon were released into waters within the Connecticut River basin, which has already been contaminated with "rock snot," which is officially called "didymo," short for its scientific name "Didymosphenia germinata."

Gillette said most of the infrastructure, including fish tanks and spillways, was underwater and buried in the mud. The facility was unreachable by road for several days and heavy equipment had to be brought in from other federal facilities as far away as Maine and New Jersey. Many of the fish escaped from the hatchery and others died. The remaining fish were evaluated for disease.

Also in the hatchery were 430,000 trout for stocking in Lake Erie and Lake Ontario. While tests showed there was no rock snot contamination in the tanks, it was determined that since the test was not 100 percent accurate, the fish should not be transported to the Great Lakes. They were used to stock waters already contaminated by rock snot.

Rock snot thrives in cold, fast-running water and populations can explode overnight, creating huge mats of material that can coat rocks and choke out other life in small rivers. Rock snot has been present in the Connecticut River since 2009. ❧

5
Rochester, Vermont

Cut off from the world, survivors improvise a bridge,
but even the dead are not safe from Irene's fury.

Irene turned Rochester, Vermont into an island on August 28, when bridges over the White River collapsed on Route 100 both north and south of the town. The old mountain road over Rochester Gap was out because Camp Brook Road, on the Bethel side, had been washed away in several places. The Route 73 bridge across the river to the west had fallen into the river and someone with a warped sense of humor had spray painted the deck with the letters "RIP."

But the real irony of the "rest in peace" graffiti lay a few thousand yards north at Woodlawn Cemetery, where a shallow stream called Mason Brook, usually only ankle deep, became a raging torrent that eroded its banks, exposing dozens of caskets and corpses, some of which washed down the stream into the highway. The brook continued across Route 100, ruining houses on the other side before finally joining the White River.

So those who managed to find their way into Rochester by foot or ATV from the south had to negotiate not only the washouts along the highway but the caskets and corpses that littered Route 100.

Mark Davis, a staff writer for the *Valley News* who visited

Photo: Wendell A. Davis Jr. (FEMA)

Irene turned sections of Rochester neighborhoods into junkyards.

Rochester in the days after Irene, wrote that the scene was "disturbing, the odor occasionally penetrating. Caskets lay open and upturned in the rubble near the brook. Nearby, another casket rested on top of a vault, slightly askew. Across Route 100, bones sat in plain sight on top of six inches of hardening mud."

Dealing with the dead, however, had to be put off while local officials dealt with the immediate problems of the survivors in this small town of just 1,100 residents. A half dozen houses had collapsed into giant piles of rubble. Other houses that had been inundated with water and mud were still standing, but uninhabitable. Phone and electric service was cut off. Nearly every road in town was washed out. Food and water were being brought in by all-terrain vehicles from Bethel, 10 miles away, over what was left of the ruined Camp Brook Road.

Landlines and cell phones stopped working so there was no contact with the outside world. Eventually, some enterprising soul realized that if you carried your cell phone up to the top of a local mountain, you could get service and assure worried friends and relatives that you were okay. After that, a constant stream of Rochester residents climbed the mountain for cell service, at least as long as the batteries held out. Many residents were unaware of what was happening in other parts of the state and that the crisis was shared by thousands.

A few days later, once the White River returned to its course, Rochester residents whose homes had been damaged or filled with mud had to deal with the dust created when several inches of toxic river water dried out and made the town look like something from the dust bowl. Residents worried that they would not be able to get food, water or fuel. How long was this going to last? When would the bridges open? Was the water safe to drink? Where was our food going to come from?

To share information in a world without phones, the residents found a wonderful solution: they went to church. Every day at 1 p.m. a town meeting was held in the Federated Church of Rochester, high on a hill, across Main Street from the town square. Crowded into the pews elbow-to-elbow, they listened to town officials and state police deliver the latest information on everything from how to keep from inhaling toxic dust to how to collect the information they would need to file insurance claims

With their refrigerators and freezers useless, the local cafe and grocery store gave their food away to grateful residents. The Huntington House on the village green and the Cafe Restaurant on Main Street joined the local convenience store and Mac's Market grocery store in the distribution of food. With freezers broken on a hot August day the food would soon spoil anyway.

"That first day, everybody was converging on the store to find out what had happened," said Beth Danforth, the manager of Mac's Market. "The road was gone in both directions. It was just horrendous. Later in the day we decided to start packing up the perishables because it was beginning to look like a long-term thing. The power was not going to come back on. It turned out our power was out for five days. We gave away the perishables but the other stuff we were still selling to people."

The store became so crowded that people could no longer fit into it, a line formed that went out the door and into the parking lot. The store had to close at dark, of course, because there was

Photo: Craig Brandon

Long lines formed outside Mac's Market as customers waited to get inside the dark store with no credit card machines.

no electricity. Credit card machines didn't work, but Danforth knew all the customers and no one was turned away for lack of cash.

Adding to the surreal atmosphere were the helicopters circling overhead. Some of these were state officials assessing the damage and others were news crews capturing the event. Later some turned out to be the National Guard, which dropped cases of bottled water onto the Village Green, and a hospital chopper that picked up several local people in need of kidney dialysis. They also brought in blankets and military style Meals Ready to Eat. The Long Trail Brewery's chopper dropped off water, diapers, food and baby food.

"The customers in the store were mostly concerned with acquiring bottled water and supplies," said Danforth. "There was some fear, but it was never chaotic. Everyone was considerate and kept their places in line. No one was panicking."

Rochester's electric substation was demolished in the flood and the lights couldn't be turned on until a portable substation was brought in by tractor trailer. When the orange Central Vermont Public Service vehicles showed up on Wednesday, they were cheered by local residents eager to get the lights back on,

Photo: Lars Gange

The force of the floodwater as it ran down hillsides in Rochester tore some houses apart while sparing adjacent houses.

Photo: Craig Brandon

The Rochester Cafe, where Heather Gorton works, gave away food and made sandwiches for survivors when the electricity failed.

which did not happen until Saturday, nearly a week after the storm. Until then, residents had to depend on Parish's Skip Mart gas pump to fuel their home electric generators. Penny Parish had to depend on her own generator to fill residents' 10-gallon cans, the total ration allowed per customer.

The sections of road that remained were layered with wreckage. Snow plows had to be used to clear them because everything was covered in two feet of silt and sand.

Shaky camera-phone videos, shot in disbelief as residents attempted to navigate their transformed town, show the once-paved surfaces now merely mud and rubble. "It looked like the water just picked up the pavement and chewed it up and spit it out," said Heather Gorton, who lives in North Hollow, across the White River from town, but works in the Cafe Restaurant on Main Street. "The river just came up and crumpled the tennis courts, it just crumpled everything up. It almost felt like a war zone," said Gorton.

"The school and church became the town center for water and food," Gorton recalled. "Because the water supply was knocked out, many people were stuck. So that was a place to go."

Elderly folks were especially challenged, as they weren't as mobile or able as others. They were also dependent upon medications, and though Rochester is home to several businesses, a drugstore is not among them. The employees of the local mountain bike store put on their boots and took to the mountain, hiking and riding over the battered terrain, collecting the much-needed medicines for the town from as far away as Rutland.

Restaurants like the one where Heather worked were trying to get rid of food as fast as they could before it spoiled in the heat.

"Anything we could cook and give away, we did. Tons of eggs," Gorton remembered. "If they wanted to buy candy or something, okay. But we were just trying to feed people. And, you know, it was cooking in the dark, because there wasn't any power. So we did what we could; we made sandwiches for people until things went bad. We had bread and eggs and milk and juices, and we ran community breakfasts for free for as long as we could. Anything we had to throw away we gave to farms, to help feed the animals. There are so many farms, and so many animals."

Photo: Craig Brandon

This damaged house at the northern end of Rochester on Route 100 was still full of mud and sitting empty six months after Irene's waters ran through it.

Photo: Lars Gange

The temporary Route 73 footbridge. Route 100 is at the top of the photo, Route 73 below.

Photo: Angela Drexel (FEMA)

The temporary footbridge from the Route 100 side, showing Route 73.

The Liberty Hill Farm had to dump all its milk because there was no way to take it to the market. Mike Bowen of the North Hollow Farm said his fields were destroyed by the toxic water, but he had hungry cows who wouldn't be taking "no" for an answer. In order to feed them, he had to carry hay bales one at a time across the makeshift footbridge. At the Kennett farm, they tried to move their cows out of the barn to higher ground but ended with the cows swimming through the water.

"At first it was surreal, like a movie —everyone was living on an adrenaline rush," Gorton recalled. "There were just so many people who could just do things, who knew how to handle things themselves, and that's how things got fixed. We're used to being protected by the mountains, but not this time."

By the time the rain stopped, nearly every one of Rochester's roads was washed out. Bridges and culverts were completely decimated, but the biggest loss was the Route 73 bridge, without which North Hollow was cut off from Rochester. "One part of a family was on one side, and the rest of the family would be across, on the other side" recalled Gorton. "They called it the 'West Rochester Island.'"

Photo: Wendell A. Davis Jr. (FEMA)

A white picket fence is all that remains standing in front of the remains of a once-lovely home in Rochester.

Faced with a problem like this, Vermonters put their heads together and came up with a series of solutions, each one better than the last. The first stage was to set up a ferry. To cross, people climbed down the steeply eroded banks of the White River and into a small boat. Passengers then pulled on a rope to get to the other side, where they hiked up the banks. "What was really amazing, though, was that people here never lost their courtesy,"

Photo: Craig Brandon

The Federated Church, high on a hill above the village green, where Rochester residents cut off from the world met each day to hear the news.

Photo: Lars Gange

Woodlawn Cemetery erosion from Mason Brook, seen from the air.

Gorton said. "They waited in line to cross."

Stage two was a giant log that was chopped to size and hauled into place to create a narrow footbridge. It was still necessary to climb down the banks on one side and back up on the other, and it was too narrow for fearful people, but at least some residents could walk from one side to the other.

The third stage was a footbridge built from the fallen ramp of the old bridge to the shore on the other side. This worked fine for pedestrians, but vehicles had to wait for the new bridge on Oct. 15, the same day that Route 100 was finally opened for its entire 216 miles down the length of Vermont. When a crane lifted the new bridge into place and down onto its abutments, Rochester residents cheered the demise of the "West Rochester Island" and held a family reunion.

When the immediate needs of the Rochester community were considered met, work began on one of Irene's most dastardly deeds: the desecration of Woodlawn Cemetery. Mason Brook had always been there, an ankle-deep tinkling brook running down the hillside through the cemetery. It was clearly marked on the original cemetery plans, and there was a little bridge built across it at the top of the hill to connect the two parts of the cemetery. In the past, its gentle trickling over the rocks had added a sense of serenity to the place.

No one, of course, had ever considered what would happen when eight feet of rain fell on a single day—and no one was there to describe exactly what happened. The ruins tell the tale. The stream flow increased by as much as fifty times its normal flow, tearing away at the banks on the stream's south side, first a little bit and then more like a landslide. As the earth fell, tombstones began to fall into the stream. Then caskets and decaying bones were disturbed, and the whole mass of bodies and dirt ran downstream, across Route 100, into the yards of the houses across the street, and finally into the White River.

It happened just a few yards from where the Route 73 bridge had collapsed. Residents could hardly believe what they were seeing. There were caskets, pieces of caskets, dead bodies and body parts on the highway and in the yards of the houses on the other side of the highway. It looked like a war zone.

In some cases, of course, the corpses and their clothing

had been separated in the flood and body parts had become separated from their caskets. Some bodies apparently came from a section of the cemetery reserved for unidentified indigents. Tom Harty, an undertaker, teacher and former state trooper, was brought in by ATV after the cemetery officials realized they were unqualified to deal with the problem. The first thing he saw on arriving was a casket sitting right on the yellow line in the middle of Route 100.

"We'll probably never know how many graves were disturbed," he said. "But my guess is about fifty. Some of the open graves were apparently from a potter's field where indigent people were buried a century ago and not recorded on cemetery records." These probably dated back to the 1860s, but at least one was so recent that it contained a modern innovation: identification papers with the name of the deceased inside a glass vial.

There were unsubstantiated reports of caskets floating down the White River all the way to White River Junction, forty miles away, but Harty said that was unlikely. "There are a lot of things that look like caskets," he said. "They may have been seeing refrigerators." Bodies did float down the White River as far as the White River Golf Course three miles away.

But the problem was a lot more difficult than collecting the remains for reburial. Determining which remains went into which grave was a dilemma worthy of a television forensics program. Harty and other volunteers gathered evidence by asking family members what the corpse was wearing at burial so they could match clothing and jewelry.

"Eventually we could account for 90 percent of the contemporary burials," Harty said, but some bones that cannot be identified will probably be reburied together with a marker identifying them with Irene's name.

"It was a difficult time for people," said Harty. "People were affected by this emotionally." Already traumatized by the direct impact of Irene, they then had to talk about dead relatives. Darlene Thompson, 40, a lifelong Rochester resident, told Wilson Ring of the Associated Press about how it felt to find out that Irene had opened up her family plot and defiled the remains of her loved ones, including her mother and father, who were found near the cemetery, and her grandmother who was found on the golf course five miles downstream. A stillborn brother and an uncle had not been found.

"Our situation has been a nightmare, but we are the lucky

Photo: Craig Brandon

Mason Brook back in its normal channel with riprap installed to help prevent future flooding.

ones," she said. "Out of five missing from our cemetery plot, the three most important ones were found."

The Vermont Health Department and a federal agency that deals with damaged cemeteries helped the Rochester Cemetery Commission put things back in order. In the meantime, blue tarps were used to cover the remains until new caskets, provided by the Vermont Funeral Directors Association, could be used to bury them again. Tarps were also laid over the edge of the cemetery that had washed away to prevent additional damage. The state medical examiner's office treated the event like a mass fatality, using DNA analysis in an attempt to identify individual bodies. The cost of restoring the washed-out section of the cemetery would be at least $1 million, according to Sue Flewelling, head of the Rochester Cemetery Commission.

By springtime, the collapsed cemetery section had been partially filled in and the brook restored to its original banks.

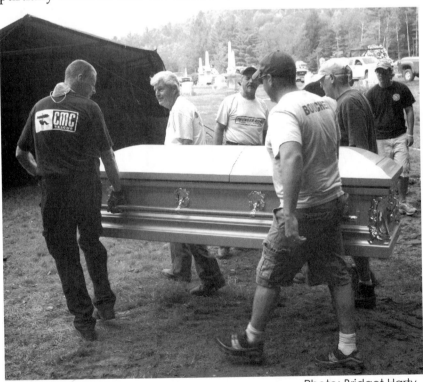

Photo: Bridget Harty

Empty caskets for reburying the bodies that floated away arrive at Woodlawn Cemetery. Tom Harty is at left.

Photo: Craig Brandon
Damage remains unrepaired six months after the storm, like this house on Route 100 at the north end of town.

A new metal frame that will eventually support the bridge over the creek was already on the site, waiting to be installed. Harty expects that more bones will be located in the coming months as fields around the river are plowed and houses are restored.

The White River Golf Course, just south of Rochester, was hit with eight feet of water that left a thick layer of silt on the fairways and twisted debris from upriver wrapped around trees. They lost more than a dozen lawn mowers, and the recovery involved picking stones out of the fairways.

Further south, in Pittsfield, with a population of only a few hundred, the historic Giorgetti Covered Bridge collapsed as well as eight homes. Irene also changed the geography of much of the town.

"You can't tell, if you weren't here before the storm," said Town Clerk Patty Haskins, "but the geography, the whole town, is really a different place—physically, you wouldn't believe how different it looks."

Pittsfield's power was out by 3 p.m. that Sunday, and phone service soon followed. By the next morning, even residents who found a way to charge their cell phones discovered there were no cell towers to support them. A handful of AT&T-powered

Photo: Craig Brandon

A house undergoing repairs on Route 100 across from the cemetery. Some of the cemetery corpses were found on this property on August 29.

phones provided the entire town with their only lines for communication, both to each other and the outside world.

"We were especially concerned about our high-risk population and all the older people," said Haskins. "We didn't want people to be stuck."

They made what plans they could and posted a notice for a town meeting. The next morning at 7:30 a.m., a group of about fifty came together to organize, sort what they knew of the situation, and set out a plan. They set up a communication center and took stock of their resources.

"There were quite a lot of firemen and medical professionals," Haskins recalled.

Her husband, Vern, and Connie Martin were part of the effort to organize a medical clinic for the town. After their assessment, it turned out that they had sixteen different medical folks on hand, from RNs to EMTs.

"You don't realize how much talent you have in a town until

they're called upon in this kind of situation," said Haskins as she listed the volunteers.

Martin worked at the Gifford Hospital and began trying to get prescription medications. Chris Masillo, a physician's assistant, took a four-wheeler to his office in Rutland and brought back medical supplies for those in need. They organized daily town meetings for everyone to check in and set up a bulletin board at the central square. This was how everyone communicated for the next several days; they posted hand-written messages and requests or offers for help. "If you had something, or needed something, you wrote a message and people knew to check in at that point," Haskins explained.

Ladders were collected so people could climb in and out of the ravines that Irene had carved into the landscape. In order to get assistance from FEMA and the National Guard, they needed to complete road assessments and send them to the state headquarters. Unfortunately, the Waterbury State Offices had already been flooded out, so when Patty Haskins first called Vermont Emergency Services, she was greeted with a recorded message. The offices had just undergone an emergency relocation to Burlington. "They said, 'Oh, just fax the road assessment up.' And I thought, now how am I going to do that?" she said. There was no phone service or electricity—and certainly no fax machine.

Up the road from the communication center, Pittsfield's Riverside Horse Farm had been hosting the wedding of Marc Leibowitz and Janina Stegmeyer before Irene hit. Though some guests set off for home early, some sixty of them, including the bridal party, were stranded in Pittsfield. "People were simply amazing," Haskins remembered. "The local people were amazing, and then there were these guests. Two guys in the wedding party were firemen, and they came down to help send the report."

Between digital cameras, generators, iPads, and cell phone tethering, they got the road assessment sent off to Burlington— the first report to be received in the state.

"Someone just walked up to me and gave me his iPhone," she said. "I didn't know what to do with that!" Still receiving limited service, the iPhone became the command center phone.

"Everyone just came together, humanity came together."

The daily meeting became an event of its own— they were fun, a time to pull together and focus on conquering new problems. "People were just hanging around Route 100. It was like a step back in time; life was moving so much slower," Haskins said.

The only traffic on VT 100 was the ATV's as road crews poured themselves into the rebuilding effort, working around the clock. With the perfect weather in the week following Irene, the sun quickly dried out road debris, creating a hazardous mess on the surface. "People came out with brooms and masks and just swept off the roads," she said. "They were covered with silt and garbage." It was nasty, but they were willing to do it.

There was a huge amount of trash throughout the town, but within minutes at town meeting, people worked together to solve the problem. "And suddenly there was garbage collection!" Haskins recalled. "No one grumbled. The local people were just incredible – the Chittenden Fire Department sent convoys over for us with pet food and home cooked meals—comfort food."

The power was out in Pittsfield from Sunday through the following Thursday, but fortunately the Pitt Stop provided a source of propane, albeit limited. Throughout the town, they shared generators as best they could. Angelique Lee, another local resident, and her husband helped to set up generators to keep the Pitt Stop running and pumping gas.

They also found a little generator to help Haskins with her town clerk's responsibilities. There was quite a lot of paperwork—and has been ever since. She was able to use the generator to run her computer and printer or the copier, but not both. It wasn't enough to power her lights, so working late into the night on the next day's agenda, she used a headlamp. One especially late night, her husband Vern came over to check on her to see when she would be finished. "Yes, I told him, but I need to trade headlamps with you because my battery is dying!" she laughed. Haskins worked 95 hours in that first week alone, and the weeks that followed weren't much shorter. "I was just running on adrenaline," she said.

One of the greatest struggles for the community, Haskins noted, has been the ongoing limbo for those who lost their homes. Displaced for months on end, many are still trying to get back

Photo: Angela Drexel (FEMA)

This Pittsfield mobile home was ripped off its foundation and broken in half by Irene's flooding.

to their community. Pittsfield lost a total of eight homes— a lot for such a small community and the personal loss these families suffered touched everyone. Since then, it hasn't been just the task of repairing homes or finding new places for these people to live that's been important, but also getting them back to their neighbors and the support network in their town. During such a trying time, the people who most need friends and help have been scattered to surrounding towns or forced to move farther away, retreating to safety with out-of-town relatives.

"It's very emotional for people, especially those who were rescued," Haskins said. Aside from all the physical damage and recovery, many of those in Pittsfield who were hit the hardest are still wading through paperwork, hanging on and hoping for some kind of help through insurance, FEMA, and relief organizations.

But everyone, no matter their situation, is trying to come back. "There's a huge sense of pride," Haskins said. "For a lot of people, they really got to be part of something. They really made a difference."

The cleanup in Pittsfield was ongoing, even months later.

Photo: Wendel Davis (FEMA)

Debris from destroyed homes is stacked for removal in front of a surviving Pittsfield house.

Belongings and pieces of homes were scattered throughout town and many precious items disappeared completely, swept away down the river. Brian Halligan, a Pittsfield home owner, lost his entire property, right down to the land itself. Friends and neighbors came to help salvage whatever they could, but bits of the house were scattered everywhere. Much of it, such as major appliances and large pieces of furniture, was never found. "It's just stuff, but all that stuff is important," Haskins noted, as she recalled walking down the riverbanks and seeing toys and clothing lodged in trees. Residents seemed hopeful that with the next spring, perhaps more belongings will be recovered.

"We have a kind of a running joke between us. If we're looking for something, a drill or snowshoes or whatever, and can't find it, we just say, 'Oh, well, that must be down the river.' Because a lot of it is," Justin Laramie laughed. His fiancée, Amy Zajdel, recalled helping to scour the riverbanks in the week after the flood and pulling whole jewelry boxes and lawn mowers out of trees intact. Unfortunately, of her belongings, the only thing they found was a piece of a practice wagon once used with their horses.

The pair had just moved to Pittsfield, leaving their farm in Mendon that May. The old property had been 36 acres of animals and activity, and moving to Pittsfield seemed like a more practical, manageable choice. They boarded their horses in Middlebury and set up a new home and a new life in a century-old house in town. The weekend Irene hit, they had friends getting married in New Jersey – a 200 person, outdoor wedding. Seeing the forecast, they prepared their home for the winds before leaving. They tied down their horse trailers outdoors, and made sure their pig and rabbits were safe. Laramie, with his Marine training, was sure to pack an emergency supply box to take along in the car – just in case.

Given the vastness of Irene, their New Jersey wedding adventure was far from the carefree weekend that had been planned. Many of the guests were delayed or unable to make it to the festivities at all, and the rain was relentless, forcing countless last-minute changes. Even so, they were unconcerned about any major effects from the water, especially at home in Vermont.

That Sunday, the day following the wedding, dawned bleak and wet in New Jersey. "The inn was leaking when we woke up," Laramie remembered. "It was just downpouring that day," Zajdel added. They had a casual breakfast but were in no rush to leave and drive home in the rain. Then the innkeeper approached to tell them that the town was about to get "shut down." He told them, "You've probably got about half an hour to get out."

They had no idea at the time, but the drive that followed was to be dangerous, frustrating, and incredibly long. Attempting to get out, they drove over lawns and through standing water, sometimes just in an attempt to keep moving. As they passed through some neighborhoods, roads were being closed just minutes after they traveled through them.

Laramie looked at Zajdel and said, "There's no turning back."

Passing mountains, they could see rainwater rushing off like waterfalls. As they attempted to cover ground in the direction of their Vermont home, obstacles seemed to emerge at every turn.

Everywhere they went, they were rerouted within minutes. They continued on, driving in circles for three hours, hitting barrier after barrier.

In the meantime, back home, friends and neighbors from Pittsfield were calling, increasingly anxious. Jane, their next-door neighbor, told them the water was rising and they were going to try to save the animals.

The pot-bellied pig, Pancetta, weighed 150 pounds and didn't even belong to Laramie and Zajdel; they were simply watching over her for friends. As the rain came down outside, she was increasingly unhappy. Their friends kept calling with updates as they tried to save her and the rabbits. While they managed to get the pig out from under the plow truck where she was hiding, the rabbits were not so lucky.

Within the course of 30 minutes, Zajdel and Laramie's drive went from struggling to navigate flooded New Jersey roads to a phone call from their friends saying, "What would be the top ten things in your life that you would want to save, if you could?"

"Our friends were out there, risking their lives for us to rescue our stuff and to help us, and there was nothing we could do, " said Laramie.

While they were stuck hundreds of miles away on a highway overpass, their friends managed to rescue their truck, trailer, and motorcycle. The water rose too fast to rescue the bunnies, the computer, or any of the treasures on the home's first floor. They received another phone call telling them that the water had risen too fast to save much; their friends had cleared out what they could. The next call was to tell them that their house was buckling and looked like it was about to be washed away. When they finally returned to Pittsfield after three straight days of travel, they found the chimney was gone and the house had sunk so low that there was no longer a door to get in; they had to climb inside through the windows. And there were no bunnies —Jane, their faithful neighbor, had buried the drowned pets before they got home.

"People just needed to see our faces," Zajdel said, when she recalled preparing to travel back to their flood-battered hometown. After eight hours of straight driving with no progress, they came to terms with the situation: it was physically

Photo: Angela Drexel (FEMA)

Piles of debris left by Irene in Pittsfield included these snowmobiles.

impossible to complete the drive that first day. They managed to stay overnight on Sunday with family in New Jersey, but knew they had to return.

"The only way to get information was social media," said Zajdel. Friends were posting photos, videos, live updates, meeting locations, and news straight to Facebook. Armed with this information and their sense of geography, they planned their route home with no knowledge of what they could expect to see in Vermont. Their family gathered extra clothes, food, water, coolers full of supplies, and backpacks for them to carry their gear. "We had no idea what the adventure would bring," Laramie remembered.

After navigating flooded highways, ATV trails, hiking trails and a barely existing path at "The Crack," where Route 4 meets VT 100 near Killington, and finally hiking down a footbridge through the middle of Route 100, they made it home to Pittsfield. "It was day three. The travel was shady, but we had to get there," Laramie said.

"The community spirit was incredible," said Zajdel. People were just loading up ATVs and backpacks and carrying supplies for whomever they could help."

Photo: Wendell Davis (FEMA)
A Pittsfield culvert, blocked by mud and debris, caused water to overflow a field and nearby structures.

They remembered the eerie emptiness of the town when they arrived; it felt like a ghost town, a shadow of what it had been just days ago. When they approached their house, their neighbor Jane didn't even recognize them.

There were mountains of mud everywhere. The garage had collapse. After three days of incredible travel and imagining, worrying, and trying to piece together cell phone pictures of what had happened, they stood in their former front yard and realized that everything had been destroyed.

"We made our top ten lists," said Laramie of their mission when they finally got inside. Everything was coated in mud, and just being in the compromised structure was a hazard. They couldn't take anything with them that was bigger than the window. Remaining possessions from the upstairs floor of the house were eventually shuttled out and put into storage.

Laramie's EMT skills were put to use immediately with a watch at the Fire Department. After that, time was a blur of searching for places to stay, attending town meetings, and figuring out what to do next. "It just didn't seem real, there were so many people stuck," Zajdel said.

Their memories of Irene, like many of their neighbors in Pittsfield and Rochester, are bittersweet. While they have pictures of Army Chinook helicopters arriving with FEMA drops, they also have fond memories of dinner out at The Crack and people setting up lawn chairs and drinking margaritas on newly formed "beaches."

"Whenever my fuel tank gets low, I get panicked, I get flashbacks," Zajdel said, recalling the intense fear during the days when supplies were uncertain and fuel delivery to their town seemed impossible. They had another wedding to attend out of state a week later, and though they were hesitant to leave, they hiked out of Pittsfield to Rutland and made it to the party, and they had a blast.

"We went through a lot together," said Laramie. "It's an inspiration; Vermont was inspiration. We were blown away by all the people who opened their doors to help. We have a fully furnished house now, thanks to the goodness of all these people. It's incredible to have family, friends, and even total strangers."

At Rochester's annual town meeting on March 5, Irene was not on the agenda, but since it was the first time everyone was in the same place since the week after Irene, people talked about it just the same. They reminded each other of the amazing rescues that firemen pulled off, about how the town had been cut off from the world, and the ingenious ways found to get across to the West Rochester Island.

Town meetings are usually held in the school auditorium, but it had not yet recovered from the flood, so it was held in the gymnasium. As the meeting was about to begin there was a call for a standing ovation for the town selectmen who had worked so tirelessly during the emergency.

When the agenda showed it was time to vote on an allocation for an emergency management fund, some wiseacre suggested they use the money to build an ark. Everyone laughed at that, but later there was silence, as if the residents were thinking maybe that wasn't such a bad idea after all. ✎

Photo: Craig Brandon

This mobile home in Wardsboro suffered a direct hit from Irene.

Photo: Craig Brandon

Glen Park in Brattleboro after the damaged mobile homes were removed.

Photo: Richard Cardonna (FEMA)

Mobile homes in a park in Conway, New Hampshire after being damaged by Tropical Storm Irene.

Mobile homes were no match for Irene

While Irene was an equal opportunity home wrecker, damaging houses of wood and brick in equal measure and even knocking down the seemingly indestructible hand-built Stone House of Woodford, Vermont selectman Steve Wright *(see chapter 4)*, one kind of structure was particularly vulnerable: mobile homes.

Hundreds of mobile homes fell victim to the storm throughout the Irene Zone, hitting areas like Williamstown, Massachusetts; Esperance, New York: and the towns of Brattleboro, Waterbury, and Berlin in Vermont particularly hard.

Built to be light and portable, mobile homes have little strength against outside pressure from water and debris. Their only defense against floods is the two-foot clearance underneath their floors that allows water to pass under them during minor flooding. When Irene attacked them with walls of water four-and even six-feet high, they simply collapsed or in some cases floated away down the rivers and streams.

Today, throughout the Irene Zone, former trailer parks

have been leveled down to the concrete pads and blocks that supported them, the electrical and water connections dangling on the ground. Other parks have struggled to rebuild. What didn't float away was so damaged that it was condemned, pulled down and hauled away to landfills, leaving residents homeless or staying with relatives. FEMA does not allow its own trailers to be erected in flooded-out mobile home parks.

Part of the problem, according to Lois Starkey, vice president for regulatory affairs for the Manufactured Housing Institute, was that as federal standards became more strict in 1976 and 2000, existing parks and trailers were "grandfathered in," and therefore exempt.

"New regulations for trailers on floodplains require building much higher," she said, "often on a metal foundation and with much better anchoring." Erecting a new trailer on a floodplain involves building a metal foundation with the floor as much as six feet above the ground.

Kevin W. Geiger, a Vermont planner, said current zoning regulations for mobile homes are the same as for other kinds of housing. In the past, he said, mobile home parks were located in floodplains because the land was cheap and couldn't be used for anything else.

"Most flood damage in Vermont occurs outside mapped flood areas, making stream setbacks critical," he said. "Flood maps are okay to poor in their accuracy."

When you understand what happened at trailer parks in the Irene Zone on August 28, it seems incredible that more people didn't die. Residents, especially elderly people, ignored warnings from firefighters and police to leave, waiting until the water was already in their living rooms. Leaving at that point meant wading through waist-deep water, and there were many unrecorded rescues as neighbors looked after their friends. The abandoned homes that did not float away had their walls smashed in.

Among the parks with dozens of ruined trailers were The Spruces in Williamstown, Massachusetts, Weston's in Berlin, Vermont, Patterson's in Duxbury Vermont., Whalley's in Waterbury, Vermont and parks along the Whetstone Brook in Glen Park, Brattleboro and the Ottauquechee River in Woodstock.

Photo: Craig Brandon

An abandoned mobile home in the Spruces Trailer Park in Williamstown, Massachusetts, after vandals removed copper and other metals for salvage.

A park in Esperance, New York had eleven homes was leveled.

In addition, since most residents of mobile homes have few financial resources, the state and local governments had to pick up the cost of cleaning up the mess. Vermont Lt. Gov. Phil Scott set up a partnership of state, private and non-profit organizations that contributed people, money and equipment to the effort.

By January, $300,000 had been raised and 68 homes demolished. It was estimated that the cost of demolishing a trailer was $2,500 per unit, but the costs increased when it was found that some of the damaged trailers contained asbestos, which required special treatment.

Another problem the former park survivors encountered was crime. Thieves took the opportunity to help themselves to the residents' belongings inside the abandoned trailers, and scam artists offered to provide demolition but instead simply scavenged the trailers for materials like copper that they could sell.

Many of the trailer survivors became homeless, living in cars or tents because the grants they received from FEMA were not enough to purchase a new home, not even a trailer. If they had the money for the down payment, lenders weren't interested. Emily Higgins of the Champlain Housing Trust helped set up a fund that would provide low interest loans to the Irene survivors using federal funds and philanthropic donations. The Vermont Legislature also passed a law waiving taxes on the purchase and sales of mobile homes.

Meanwhile, at The Spruces park in Williamstown, scores of damaged and abandoned trailers lined up in rows were not removed because the state and the owners of the trailer park were in court battling over who would pick up the bill. (*See chapter 6.*) ✎

6
Williamstown & Greenfield, Mass.

A pink artist studio floats away, and a haunted covered bridge gets a last-minute reprieve.

When Tropical Storm Irene pushed the flooded Hoosic River over a berm into the Spruces Mobile Home Park in Williamstown, Massachusetts on August 28, no one could have predicted the chain of events that led to what six months later looked like a 113-acre migrant camp right in the heart of one of New England's most upscale college towns.

Before August 28, the park was home to some 300 senior citizens, many of them in their 70s and 80s, and on fixed incomes, who enjoyed the low rent and the willingness of the park owners to let them keep their cats and dogs, something many retirement homes prohibited. The park had flooded a number of times before, and many residents refused firefighters' orders to evacuate until the water was lapping at their front steps.

Carol Zingarelli, one of the residents who evacuated and assumed she would be back the next day, described the disoriented senior citizens who wandered around in a daze at the schoolhouse evacuation center while their pets fought each other in the hallways.

"The animals were freaking out," she said, "but their owners were keeping to themselves, not really talking with anyone, waiting until they could go home." Later that night, she was

121

Photo: Craig Brandon

The elegant giant lions that guard the gates of the Spruces Mobile Home Park on Route 2 in Williamstown hide the devastation that lurks just a few hundred feet away.

able to take a look at her trailer, but only from a distance because police and firemen had sealed off the park and were not letting anyone in.

"I could see the water up to the windows in the rec hall," she said. She spent several days in a motel until her money ran out, and then stayed in several locations chosen by the local Red Cross. Meanwhile, her trailer her been "red tagged," condemned by building inspectors, just like three-quarters of the 225 units crowded into the park. After several months, she was able to acquire a different trailer in the park that had been abandoned by its former owner after the park became a disaster area.

"I think I handled it all pretty well, but I only know that because I saw so many people around me who weren't handling it well," she said. "Everybody seems to be living in fear because no one knows what is going to happen. A lot of people are depressed. There's a lot of forgetfulness. We don't have the vibrant neighborhood we had before. There's a sadness and a cloud hanging over us."

Six months after Irene, 159 of the 225 trailers are still uninhabitable, but few have been demolished. Instead they are lined up, row upon row, with broken windows, insulation hanging out of holes in the walls, waterlogged particle board rotting, debris strewn around the yards and full of black mold that has grown up the sides of the trailers and onto the roof. The major problem that has halted demolition work is a lawsuit filed against the town and the state by the owners of the park, Morgan Management, which fears it is being forced into bankruptcy. The cleanup costs are so high that the company can no longer make a profit and wants to walk away from the mess and let the state, local and federal governments handle the cleanup. While lawyers fight it out in court, the residents of the Spruces are in limbo.

"It's an old park, built in 1954, and the trailers are so old that they're not worth anything," said Robin Lenz, coordinator of Higher Ground, a support group set up by local church groups to deal with the problems at the Spruces. Even those who received FEMA grants did not receive enough to demolish their trailers.

Photo: Craig Brandon

What Irene didn't destroy in the flood was vandalized by fraudulent workers who stripped the metal off and left.

Photo: Craig Brandon

Row after row of condemned trailers are lined up in the park six months after Irene, while the park owners and government argue in court over who will pay the cost of the cleanup.

The few that survived the flood are standing among other trailers, less than 10 feet away, that are empty and full of mold.

"Our town realizes we have a tragedy and a disaster here," she said. "We are working hand in hand, but it is a slow process." Before the flood, she said, few people in Williamstown (population 6000) had any idea how many low income people lived in the trailer park with the lions in front of it at the eastern town line.

That leaves the elderly residents, or "Sprucies" as they call themselves, in the middle of a park with trailers that are neither being renovated nor removed. Many of the residents complained about allergies caused by all the mold, and many worry that the park will never return to its former state.

To add insult to injury, many of the damaged mobile homes were burglarized in the months following the storm. Scam artists who offered to tear down damaged homes actually ended up taking the aluminum skins and copper pipes for their own use and left the open carcasses behind. Police Chief Kyle Johnson had at least nine reports of larcenies in the park but admitted that no one had been caught and there were few leads. Among the items taken were a refrigerator, a power washer, a flagpole with a flag, a gas stove and eight lightbulbs. As more people were able to return to the park, the larcenies seemed to decrease, said David Rebello, vice president of the Spruces Tenants Association. "We went through this disaster and now we have to watch for crooks taking advantage of us," he said.

North Adams, the next town to the east, was getting three 911 calls per minute during the height of the storm, beginning at 10 a.m. on Sunday. The evacuation center for residents with flooded houses had to be moved from Drury High School to the St. Elizabeth Parish Center because of flooding on Church and Ashland streets. But the greatest road damage was farther east, beyond the sharp turn on Route 2 known as the "hairpin turn" that leads to one of the most beautiful drives in New England.

In 1914, at the dawn of the automobile era, the Mohawk Trail was one of the first designated scenic drives in America, following an old Indian trail for 65 scenic miles from Orange to Williamstown in Massachusetts along the Cold, Millers and

Photo: Alberto Pilot (FEMA)

FEMA Individual Assistance Officer Reginald Burt, right, conducts a property damage assessment in the basement of a North Adams home.

Photo: Mass DOT

The Mohawk Trail collapsed into the Cold River and bridge abutments were washed out as Irene drove the water up over the road.

Photo: Mass DOT

Deerfield Rivers. The highway through the Berkshires and the Hoosac Range of mountains was added to the National Register of Historic Places in 1973, and each autumn thousands of tourists drive along the trail or stare out the windows of tourist-oriented leaf-peeping buses at the colorful displays.

On August 28, however, Irene became one of the worst vandals the trail had ever experienced, dumping eight inches of rain on the headwaters, causing a flash flood that wiped out roads and bridges, creating landslides along highways, and finally threatening the scenic Bridge of Flowers in Shelburne Falls and a historic covered bridge in Greenfield.

But the hardest hit area, by far, was the six miles of the Mohawk Trail between Florida to the west and Charlemont in the east where the highway twists and turns in an area known to locals as the "dead man's curves," with a steep embankment on one side and a series of rocky outcroppings on the other. On August 28 the embankment and some of the roadway collapsed into the river, sending trees, brush, rocks and earth over the pavement. While some of the paved road remained, highway experts feared that it was so undercut by the raging river that it was no longer safe. The containment walls designed to hold back the earth from the highway were torn and twisted.

The Mohawk Trail was closed after Irene. State highway officials who had explored the damage on foot and on all-terrain vehicles estimated that it might take years to repair the damage. First, a temporary road would have to be constructed so heavy equipment could bring in the thousands of tons of gravel, rock and soil needed to repair the embankments. Then the road would have to be repaved and inspected before cars would be able to use one of the state's main tourist arteries connecting the Berkshires to the Pioneer Valley.

The Cold River, usually a fast-running but narrow stream, overflowed its banks onto the highway causing slope failures, undermining the pavement and creating instability along the banks. Bridge approaches were eroded and retaining walls were damaged before mud slides covered the highway with tons of dirt and rock. In one spot, near mile marker 25, the river created a new bed where the road used to be.

About 2,400 vehicles use the highway every day, the state

estimated, so the state highway department put the project on a fast track and divided it into three contracts, awarded them to three construction companies and set an aggressive timetable, vowing that the road would be open in December. An expedited bidding process was set up and plans were drawn up in just three weeks, a process that normally takes as long as a year.

At first, flashing signs on Interstate 91 warned motorists away from Route 2. and drivers had to make a 36-mile detour that added 20 minutes to a trip from Greenfield to Williamstown. Charlemont business owners complained that the signs were misleading because the road was actually open to their town, so

Photo: Mass DOT

Even though it was given top priority and put on a fast track, it took construction workers three and a half months to repair the damage that Irene had done in just eight hours.

Photo: Mass DOT

The rebuilding contract was divided into three parts, each one going to a separate construction company.

the state took the signs down. The portion of the road between Charlemont and Florida was closed for three months while construction went on day and night, seven days a week through rain and snowstorms.

Finally at 9 a.m. on December 15, a ceremony was held at the entrance to the Mohawk State Forest Campground to complete what the Department of Transportation called "an unprecedented effort" that took 14 weeks and $23 million.

"Had the work been completed under a regular construction schedule, it would have taken an entire construction season to complete," said Sara Lavoie, spokesperson for the transportation department. Even an October snowstorm that shut down schools and highways caused work to stop for only a few hours.

"There will be some work that continues on retaining walls next year," said Lavoie, "but it will have no effect on traffic."

Towns along the Mohawk Trail struggled to get their town roads open as well. The town of Florida estimated it would spend $3 million on its roads, a third more than the town's entire annual budget. In Clarksburg the price tag was set at $1 million and in North Adams it was $5 million.

In the Deerfield River town of Charlemont, halfway between Williamstown and Greenfield on the Mohawk Trail, the river rushed across the highway and into the basement of the Mohawk Park Restaurant and Pub. A huge sinkhole opened up in the picnic area among the tourist cabins. The Hawlemont Regional School was damaged, delaying the opening of classes for its 100 students. Electrical circuits and the school's boiler were damaged and there was some question about the well that supplied water to the school, but help arrived in the form of students from the Charlemont Academy, who donned face masks and gloves and used shovels to remove the thick covering of silt from the baseball field. Some of the students said the muck was like Jell-O, difficult to collect on a shovel without it sliding off. The town's emergency command center, normally located in the fire station, had to be moved to town hall when the water level in the firehouse began to rise.

Photo: Eric Dean

Charlemont residents explore the damages to the Mohawk Trail.

Photo: Eric Dean
The driver of this car had to be rescued from this road in Charlemont.

Charlemont is also the home of Zoar Outdoor, which runs whitewater rafting tours on the Deerfield River. Kevin Miller, director of guided programs, and a person who knows the river well, said Irene made significant changes to its course and the embankments. Most of these, he said, would make for more interesting tours in the future. A barn full of Zoar's equipment floated down the Deerfield, including life jackets, paddles, pumps and helmets. Pieces of the building ended up in nearby trees, but within a few days they were back in business using equipment borrowed from other companies. The self-guided tours were cancelled because the river was still flowing in ways that were considered too unpredictable and dangerous. Launch points were also moved farther downstream.

The Olde Willow Restaurant on the Deerfield River in Charlemont was spared from the flood when the river crossed the highway, but a six-foot-deep sinkhole opened up in the parking lot, making it impossible for customers to enter. After waiting in vain for someone to come and help her, Ellen Hartwig, the restaurant's elderly owner, put up a hand-printed cardboard sign that said simply "Please Help Me." Within days, passersby noticed her sign and notified the C.D. Davenport Construction and Trucking Co., which sent six truckloads of gravel to fill in the hole.

One of the prime tourist destinations along the Mohawk Trail is the Bridge of Flowers, a former trolley bridge over the Deerfield River that connects the two parts of Shelburne Falls. Built in 1908, it has since been covered in plantings by local gardeners. The Deerfield River, which had already damaged Wilmington, Vermont, further upstream, had picked up water from tributaries and rose to cover the bridge's deck. Local residents crowded along the rail and stood in the rain fearing the hundred-year-old bridge was about to collapse. Locals still talk about what they saw that day, a river that normally ran thirty feet below the bridge seemed to have become possessed by a demon—chocolate brown, rolling and churning with white caps as it raced by, carrying parts of houses, entire trees, bits of lumber and propane tanks.

One resident with a video camera caught the moment that the river pulled a pink house off its foundation on Conway Street and dragged it across to the other side of the street, where it came to rest against a maple tree, creating sparks as its electrical connection was pulled away. The building was the studio of renowned quilter Ann Brauer, who was at a craft show in Chicago on August 28. After calls from friends she watched her studio's demise on YouTube.

Brauer, 62, of Ashfield purchased the former video store in the 1990s and painted it bubblegum-pink to make it distinctive. Her quilts are regularly displayed at craft shows and have price tags as high as $5,000. Although she had her best work with her,

Photo: Craig Brandon

The sign for Indian Plaza on the Mohawk Trail. Behind it and beyond the pile of debris is the Olde Willow Restaurant.

Photo: Craig Brandon

The Indian Plaza tourist stop was inundated with four feet of water that came over Route 2 from the Deerfield River across the street.

she lost many more quilts to the river, as well as her "stash" of personally selected fabrics and her sewing machines, which were covered in mud. When she arrived in Shelburne Falls after the flood, she found her studio resting partially on the pavement of Conway Street. Before it was demolished and she relocated, her grandmother's quilts, the ones that inspired her work, were rescued from an upstairs room in the pink building.

When the waters finally receded on Monday morning, Shelburne Falls residents were glad to see that both the pedestrian bridge and the metal auto bridge had survived, but both were a mess, covered in silt and mud. The stone dust that paved the pedestrian path down the middle of the Bridge of Flowers had been washed away. Yellow caution tape closed off both ends of the bridge, but the flowers on the sides continued to bloom in the bright sunshine. The town had to pour 25,000 pounds of stone dust to repair the path, but an inspection found that the Bridge of Flowers was not seriously damaged.

The surrounding town, however, was not so lucky. An estimated 300 residents of Shelburne Falls, many on Conway Street, had to be evacuated; their houses were seriously damaged. Water entered many of the businesses on State and Bridge Streets. Next to the Bridge of Flowers, the Iron Bridge that carries vehicle traffic between the two sides of the village, was damaged and remained closed until engineers had a chance to examine it.

Building inspector James Hawkins spent part of Sunday and all day Monday examining the rows of shops and described what he found as "epoch damage." All of the buildings were structurally sound, he said, but electrical panels, furnaces and oil tanks in basements were damaged. The floodwaters inundated the quaint shops on State Street on the west side of the river with as much as four feet of water. A few of them, such as the Brush with Fate art gallery— temporarily renamed "One Hell of a Brush with Fate"—were still closed six months later.

Colrain artist Jo-Ann Sherburne, who operated a framing shop and art gallery at 40 State Street, was able to reopen the framing shop, but the art gallery needed more work. She used her savings because the loans she qualified for required extensive paperwork and carried rates that were too high. With no money

Donated photo

The raging Deerfield River roiled and churned through Shelburne Falls. At its peak it was actually flowing over the top of the Bridge of Flowers.

Photo: Craig Brandon

How the bridge and river looked under more normal circumstances.

coming in during the renovations, she said, times were hard but were brightened a bit by her neighbors. Even if they didn't have the resources to buy anything, she said, they offered emotional support and reassurance that she was not alone in her hardship.

Paul St. Martin, owner of the West End Pub, was able to reopen in November, but his other business, the Cafe Martin, closed when the lease ran out. He didn't have flood insurance, he said, because the premium was too high. He lost five freezers full of food when the electricity went out, as well as all of his liquor, his furnace, air conditioning and a basement bathroom.

On Monday morning, just as residents began to clean up the mess, the town imposed an emergency water restriction because of damages to the pumping station. Water was to be used only for consumption and hygiene, which didn't include hosing out all the mud.

Shelburne Falls Booksellers was back in business at a new location just six weeks after Irene dumped three feet of silt and toxic water into the old shop. Mike Muilenberg, one of the owners, said about three-quarters of the vintage and antiquarian books in the shop were damaged beyond repair and went to the landfill. The other 25 percent went to the new store, along with art and prints from the old store's walls. Among the losses were rare local history books. The owners are looking for people who have such books that they would like to sell.

On Monday morning, Shelburne Falls survivors packed into the Foxtown Restaurant to swap stories and share news. With both bridges closed, Shelburne Falls became a divided community and it took miles of driving to get from one side of town to the other.

Beryl MacAdam, who had lived on Conway Street for 53 years, evacuated on Sunday morning when the water crossed the road and was lapping at her driveway. When she returned on Monday she found the house flooded with water. Even her car, which was stored in a garage, was full of water. Later on Monday her family helped her move her possessions out of the house.

To help residents and business owners cope with the stress caused by Irene, a group of homeopaths set up a free clinic to deal with the nightmares, sleeplessness and anxiety attacks. Dale

Photo: Craig Brandon

Bald Mountain Pottery was one of many boarded-up shops remaining on State Street in Shelburne Falls six months after the flood, but most businesses returned, sometimes in new locations.

Moss, one of the organizers, said people in Shelburne Falls were suffering some of the symptoms of Post-Traumatic Stress Disorder.

The Iron Bridge that carries cars across the Deerfield River was closed for a month while state inspectors examined the damage. When the yellow caution tape was finally removed on September 24, local business owners and pedestrians cheered it as another step toward normal.

The town of Colrain became a series of islands isolated from each other as roadways were washed out, but just before the storm the town's police officers and firefighters were stationed in various places around town, not just at the station, making it easier to send help where it was needed.

On August 28 they rescued a man who was trapped in his car by floodwaters. The raging waters pushed the officer back during the first rescue attempt. After that, the driver was able to restart the car and drove it to higher ground. An elderly woman trapped in her house across from the flooded state highway garage was rescued after waist-deep water flooded her house.

Joanne Deady was on the phones at Colrain's Emergency Operations Center in the fire station on August 28, when the calls began to come in fast and furious. Wires were down. Bridges were out. People wanted to know which roads were flooded and which were still open. Others asked my basement is flooded, what should I do? How much more rain are we going to get? Later in the emergency she was making calls herself, looking for buildings that could serve as shelter for the storm's refugees.

Then volunteers passing in and out began telling her about her mobile home on Main Road, where she had lived for 28 years. The water, she was told, was up to the front door. At 1 p.m. she was given a ride by the police chief to see for herself. When she arrived she found the water hip-deep inside; the trailer had been pushed off its foundation and four feet to one side, and was now resting at an angle.

When FEMA inspectors had a chance to look at it later that week, they determined that the frame was twisted and the trailer was written off as a total loss. Nearly everything inside, furniture, appliances, an organ and four guitars and their clothing had to be thrown out as well because it had been in contact with the toxic water. She and her husband, Howard, and their bulldog Caesar had to move in with her brother. They filled out insurance claims and FEMA forms so they could get back on their feet.

On nearby Roberts Lane, Samantha and Scott Roberts watched as the East River Branch swept over its banks and began filling their basement and then seeped up through the floor. They moved their vehicles to higher ground and packed up their personal items before heading to a neighbor's house. They had about 20 minutes to get to safety.

When they were able to return they found that 160 bales of hay had been swept away. Guard rails on the road had been twisted out of shape like some kind of modern sculpture. They lost most of their corn crop, and about a third of their pasture land was covered with mud.

Among the refugee families forced to live in tents were Jeff and Christina Sullivan of Main Road, Colrain. The North River destroyed their white ranch house, which had been in Christina's family for four generations. "I was more worried about the wind

Photo: Alberto Pilot (FEMA)

Tho Do, an individual assistance officer from FEMA, assists a couple from Shelburne Falls with a claim.

when I heard reports before the storm hit," she told reporter Anita Philips of the *Greenfield Recorder*. The couple had to move in with her parents and their two sons.

All six of them managed to escape uninjured and spent a week in a tent on Sullivan's aunt's lawn before they moved into a pop-up camper nearby. "There are six of us staying in there," Christina said. "We left our home with one suitcase and a couple of necessities and that's it. We lost everything else." Their sons, Gabriel, 8, and Austin, 7, still feel the aftereffects of the disaster.

"They both worry every time they hear there might be rain," she said."They think this will happen again. The world as they knew it is gone. Kids shouldn't have to worry. They should be kids."

When they toured the property of their condemned home later, Gabriel found a baseball bat half-buried in the flood. Fish were swimming in a pool that had formed under the front porch and the property smelled like a beach after the tide goes out. The former yard was filled with debris and pieces of destroyed sheds and oil tanks. A flat-screen television was found facedown near the front door. The children's swing set had been washed fifty feet downstream, near the Sullivans' ruined trash compactor. When they opened the back door the smell of mildew hit them. Inside, the watermark on the wall showed that the water had come up five to six feet.

"We know that we have to start over," said Jeff Sullivan, "we're just not sure how we're going to do that."

In Conway, a brand-new retaining wall built to hold back the South River was washed away by Irene. Designed to be ecologically friendly, the wall had provided space for plantings and shade trees to keep the water cooler for fish, but it was no match for the flash flood. The wall did not extend around a corner of Pumpkin Hollow Brook, allowing the powerful water to get in behind it. A month later, the town completed a $150,000 replacement wall that was less beautiful but more functional, designed to take the next Irene that comes to call. They used gravel and four-foot chunks of rock this time.

In Buckland, one of the hardest-hit areas, roads, culverts, sidewalks, bridges, utility poles and sewer lines were broken. Damage was estimated at $18.5 million by FEMA and $25 to $30 million by an engineer hired by the selectmen. Loans and grants from the state and federal government were expected to cover much of this cost, but the repairs would take many months. Guardrails had been washed out along Clesson Brook Road and residents were worried about cars slipping into the stream when the weather got colder. Other houses along the brook were now so close to the water that they feared their houses would slip into it during the spring floods.

The Old Hawley Bridge was destroyed and extensive damage to the Clesson Brook and Apple Valley sections of town was caused by debris that washed downstream and became caught in culverts and bridge abutments, diverting the water out of the streambed and toward residential areas. Getting rid of all that debris, the selectmen said, was difficult because of laws restricting work in wetlands and streambeds. Local owners of heavy equipment were willing to do the work themselves, including removing debris from streambeds but were told by the town that this could endanger their FEMA grants.

The town also received a grant to cover a portion of Conway Street where sidewalks, pavement and several homes were heavily damaged and a small quilt shop was washed 100 feet downstream. Dirt roads had been turned into mud and selectmen were concerned that once school reopened the buses would have trouble on the narrower roads. Even important projects that were given top priority had to be delayed because contractors were so busy in other towns.

In Leyden, Laura Moriarty and Robert Barry lost nearly all their belongings when the Green River swept away their unique octagonal home on West Leyden Road. It had a spiral staircase, mosaics on the walls and stained glass windows. At 9 a.m. on August 28, Robert looked out the window and saw how fast the river, just 12 feet away, was rising.

"We thought we had a bit of time to pack things up," Moriarty told *Greenfield Recorder* reporter David Rainville. "We got a few of the kids' clothes and some other things. Bob tried to go back into the house, but it was apparent that there wasn't time. Water had started coming into the house. It would've been moving too fast for him to get back safely."

They carried their childern, Liam, 2, and Ashlyn, 10, to safety as well as a laundry hamper full of their clothes, four kittens, and the mother cat, Cadillac Escalade, and went to a friend's house in Turners Falls where they stayed temporarily. An hour later, Barry realized they had forgotten to bring Ashlyn's medicine, so he went back to Leyden, but by then the house was gone. All that was left was Ashlyn's second-story bedroom, which was sitting against a shed attached to a carport. The rest of the house had been lifted up by the river and smashed to pieces against the Ten Mile Bridge.

"We expected to come back to a flooded house," said Moriarty. "We never in a million years expected it to smash into a bridge. Pieces of the siding and timbers from the house were embedded in the bank and some pieces were caught high in the branches of trees along the river. Some residents of Leyden have gathered our clothes and our belongings they've found along the river. They've been washing our clothes and leaving our things in the one room of the house that's left." Also left there were family photographs they thought they had lost.

"We lost hundreds of photos, that was the worst," said Moriarty. "We have about six that people found and returned. They're in rough shape but could probably be touched up." They also lost scrapbooks she had made for the children and their toys, some of which went back three generations.

Despite their losses, Moriarty and Barry said they consider themselves lucky that so many friends were able to help them after their disaster. "Everyone we've run into has done whatever they can to help us. People have been phenomenal." After spending time at the Quality Inn, the family moved to an unfurnished apartment in Buckland, where they are beginning to feel the joy of something close to normal. "Having a Rubbermaid trash can is moving up in the world," said Barry. "Now our trash isn't just a bag on the floor. We're re-entering the twenty-first century as fast as we can."

But memories of the disaster will not fade quickly. "Liam has been hit the hardest by this," Moriarty said. "He's very confused, you can see it in his face. We have to drive by (the location of the old house) to take Ashlyn to school, and he keeps saying 'home, home.' It's heartbreaking. How do you explain it to a two-year-old? Ashlyn is our little trooper. She's taking it well."

"We're really fortunate," said Barry. "I've heard of people living in tents on their property. I'm grateful we had some savings. Otherwise we'd be staying in a shelter or living in a tent ourselves."

Interstate 91, the major north-south highway in the Pioneer Valley, was closed for a week while bridge inspectors examined the footings and supports of a bridge that carried it over the Deerfield River. Scuba divers examined the underwater bridge piers, but the job had to be delayed for a day when the raging waters made diving unsafe. Eventually repairs were made to the southbound span, but thousands of cars were detoured through Greenfield and Deerfield along Routes 5 and 10, creating massive traffic jams. This turned out to be a bonus for local businesses, including the Yankee Candle Co., which reported that it was doing a record business from all the cars creeping along the highway.

Photo: Mass DOT

Heavy equipment is used to clear the riverbed under the southbound lane of Interstate 91 at the Deerfield River crossing.

Irene turned the valuable and productive farmland at the Williams Farm on Mill Village Road in Deerfield into a 75-acre desert. Owner Kenneth Williams said it looked like a beach when the water receded. Nearly two months after the storm, it took another month for a half-dozen earth moving vehicles to remove tons of sand, at places three feet deep, deposited by the flooded Deerfield River. That allowed the buried topsoil to come to the top again. The sand was pushed onto a narrow strip along the river. The water was estimated to have risen ten feet above the ground and left behind fallen trees, propane tanks and other debris that floated down the river on August 28. The cost of the work came to $5,000 an acre or a total of $375,000. Also lost was a 1,200-foot irrigation system worth $60,000. All of this damage, Williams pointed out, took place in just ten hours.

A number of charities were set up to help farmers, including the Deerfield-based Community Involved in Sustaining Agriculture, which distributed funds donated by Equity Trust and Whole Foods Market. The $10,000 loans don't seem like much when farmers are facing a quarter-million-dollar loss, but Williams said every bit helps. Without this kind of assistance local farmers could go out of business faced with the loss of all their crops and the damage caused by Irene. State Agricultural Commissioner Scott Soares said the farms along the Deerfield River in Franklin County had some of the best soils in the world and were among the hardest hit in the state.

In Deerfield, Town Administrator Bernard Kubiak said the town has depended on agriculture as the basis of its economy since the seventeenth century, but Irene washed away the topsoil from farms and replaced it with sand, grit and gravel washed down in the Deerfield River from as far away as Vermont. "It's a year's worth of work wiped out. It makes you want to cry." At Pioneer Gardens, owner Jaap Molenaar said the flooding destroyed two acres of ornamental crops like daylilies. About 18 to 20 acres of his land was covered with silt and mud.

Nathan L'Etoile, assistant commissioner of the Massachusetts Department of Agricultural Resources, said a potato farm in Hatfield lost 300 acres and a Deerfield farm lost 50 acres of vegetables. Dairy farmers had to dump milk because the collection trucks could not reach them over the damaged roads.

In just a few hours, Irene caused $13 million in damages in the town of Greenfield, where the Mohawk Trail crosses Interstate 91, including damage to the town's water supply dam and $3 million in bridge damage. There was also erosion damage at the Newton School and on Mead Street and retaining walls were damaged at a park.

The sewage treatment plant was inundated by flood waters from the Green River and shut down Sunday afternoon, allowing raw sewage to be dumped into the river just before it emptied into the Connecticut, making life even more miserable for everyone dealing with the flood farther downstream. The state Department of Public Health advised everyone downstream to avoid boating, fishing, kayaking and swimming, but many of those downstream residents were dealing with water running into their houses. Exposure to sewer bacteria can cause gastrointestinal ailments such as vomiting and diarrhea as well as respiratory effects.

Water reached the middle of the third floor of the four-story

Photo: Craig Brandon

The Eunice Williams Covered Bridge as it looked in March 2012. The railing is still hanging off the side, but the edge at the left is no longer hanging free. It has been shored up with a new abutment. The Green River, which was flowing around the bridge to the left after the storm, has been restored to its normal course under the bridge.

treatment building. For two days the plant remained underwater while engineers used pumps to remove the water and restart the chlorine process to begin treating the waste before it entered the river, but the plant was not restored to full function for six weeks.

"The storm was catastrophic," said Sandra Shields, director of the Greenfield public works department. "In all my years here I have never seen anything like it."

On first inspection, it seemed that Irene had finally brought an end to the long life of the historic Eunice Williams Covered

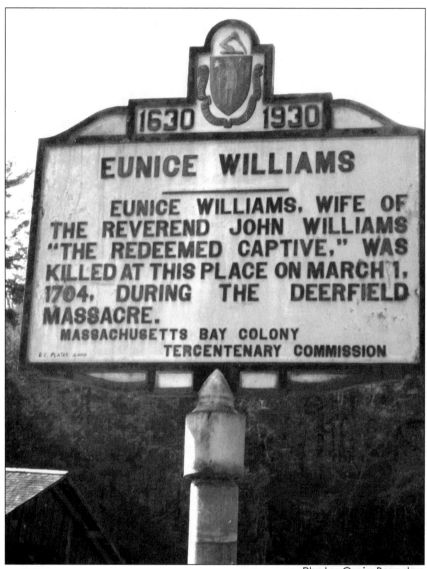

EUNICE WILLIAMS

EUNICE WILLIAMS, WIFE OF THE REVEREND JOHN WILLIAMS "THE REDEEMED CAPTIVE," WAS KILLED AT THIS PLACE ON MARCH 1, 1704, DURING THE DEERFIELD MASSACRE.
MASSACHUSETTS BAY COLONY
TERCENTENARY COMMISSION

Photo: Craig Brandon
The historical marker at the bridge, the top of which can be seen at lower left.

Bridge. It was hanging out over the river after one abutment was destroyed and it was in danger of collapse. The raging Green River had carved a new course around the bridge and Shields was afraid that when it fell down, it would dam up the river and destroy the town's water pumping facility just downstream.

"But after the water went down we could see that the bridge was not in as precarious a state as we thought," she said. "This was a bridge that had a lot of sentimental value to the town, so we started looking for a way to save it."

Originally built in 1870, the bridge was named after Eunice Williams, who died in an Indian raid at that spot on the Green River in 1704. Many New England ghost hunters claim that the ghost of Williams still haunts the bridge. It was destroyed by fire in 1969, but a replacement was dedicated in 1972. Sometime after 2000, it was closed to vehicles because inspectors discovered it was warping and slowly being torn apart.

The cost to demolish the bridge was set at $75,000, three-quarters of which would be paid for by FEMA, but Shields said it was clear that most people in the town wanted the bridge preserved and plans were drawn up to not only save the bridge, but also make it strong enough for cars to use.

Kenneth Block, a former town engineer who had a minor role in the construction of the current bridge, made a close inspection of the damage and reported back to Shields that saving the bridge was not only reasonable but also cost effective. When he examined the truss system under the bridge he found it was made from Douglas Fir, a high-quality wood shipped in from California. While there was damage to the siding, railings and walkway, the trusses were sound and "straight as an arrow." Saving it would be as simple as jacking it up so the abutments could be repaired and then lowering the bridge back down onto them. It could then open to bicycles and pedestrians, but to open it for vehicular traffic would take more reinforcement.

Over the winter, workers poured tons of gravel into the riverbed that Irene carved around the bridge, forcing the river back into its proper channel under the bridge. At the same time temporary abutments were installed to stabilize the bridge and keep it from hanging loose over the river. Eventually construction crews will rebuild the permanent abutments and restore the road to the bridge.

While New York and Vermont got most of the media attention, Irene did millions of dollars worth of damage in western Massachusetts along the Mohawk Trail, including damaged property and lost tourist revenue. ✍

Photo: Hans Pennick (FEMA)
The hallway in a house in Schoharie, New York, infested with mold.

Mold: The silent destroyer Irene left behind

When Irene survivors returned to their homes after the waters began to recede, they found damaged foundations, furniture that had been tossed and jumbled as if a giant with a temper had been there, and ruined family treasures like photo albums and antiques.

What they didn't see right away was the impact that black mold would have on their futures. The mold thrives on wet cellulose and loves sheetrock and particle board. Left alone, black mold, or *stachybotrys* to use its scientific name, grew up the walls of damaged houses until it reached the ceiling and the two sides met.

The only cure for it was demolition, using sledge hammers to rip out the sheetrock to the high water mark, which could be four to eight feet high. Dr. Joseph Laquatra, a mold specialist from Cornell, said in most cases homeowners could do it themselves as long as they followed guidelines, but others might want to hire a certified remediation contractor and use a special moisture meter on damaged walls. Anyone removing mold should wear a mask, he added.

Black mold can make people sick, especially those with an allergy to it. ◁

7
Woodstock, Vermont

*A landmark covered bridge is damaged and an
underwater newspaper preserves its long tradition.*

P atrick Crowl, owner of the Woodstock Farmer's Market on
Route 4, thought August 28 was going to be nothing worse
than a rainy day. "It didn't even really appear to be raining
that hard," he said.

Then he received a phone call no business owner ever wants.
A friend driving on Route 4 called him at his home in Pomfret,
nestled on a hill high above the Ottauquechee River. He needed
to get to the market; things weren't looking good. By the time he
arrived, Route 4 had been closed due to the rapidly rising water,
and parts of it had already collapsed.

"By the time we got there it was apparent that there was a
major catastrophe in the making," he said. "As we arrived, we
saw that the dumpster was floating in the parking lot. Route
4 had been closed for half an hour. We didn't really have a lot
of choices. We managed to park on higher ground and waded
down to the store to try to figure out what to do."

With more than the standard fare for a market of its size,
Crowl's store stocks gourmet grocery items alongside farm-fresh
produce in addition to an in-house bakery and deli packed with
tasty treats. The shelves of goods and bins of produce stretch
from floor to ceiling. When Crowl entered the store that day, the

Photo: Woodstock Farmer's Market

The Ottauquechee River, which normally flows behind these buildings, overflowed to cover Route 4 on August 28.

Photo: Woodstock Farmer's Market

The next day the waters receded a bit, but Route 4 was still blocked.

Photo: Woodstock Farmer's Market

When workers got inside the Farmer's Market, this is what they found in the back room.

clock was against him and the water was already ankle-deep.

"My first thought was to get the computer up off the ground, but then you quickly realize that the water is rising so fast that you have moments to grab things from downstairs and get everything out," he said. But how can you even begin? Rescuing food and wares was out of the question—there was simply too much to carry. With the water rising and conditions rapidly worsening, Crowl was forced to make a tough call. They needed to go. "We had to abandon ship, it was that bad," he said. "We just had to hope for the best."

They shut off the power and turned to go back home, but even that was out of the question.

"The water was rising, it was halfway up the door. And when we opened up the door to leave, it was like opening the door to a ship or a submarine, with the water just rushing in. We couldn't go home because we couldn't get home, so we stayed with some friends. We just watched the water, there was nothing else to do."

When he returned early on Monday morning, the water was gone, but four and a half feet of rushing mud and debris had ravaged his equipment and displays, shattering and twisting and turning heavy pieces of furniture over or even upside down. What remained was ten inches of thick mud mixed with everything from ripe tomatoes to papers to jars of jam and bags of chips. Mounds of fruits and vegetables, caked in mud, continued to ripen under Monday's beautiful sunshine. Broken signage, remnants of baskets that once held potatoes and green peppers, and bits of other wares lay scattered in the wake of a giant's temper tantrum. It was daunting.

That first day was muddy, stressful and unavoidable. "Everybody wanted to help, which was great, but we didn't know where to begin," Crowl recalled. "You don't have training for this."

So they began at the beginning, hauling things out and throwing them in the parking lot. At first they attempted to separate what could be kept from what was ruined, but there was very little to salvage.

"We had umpteen million dumpsters come, and we just carried it all out to the parking lot. You just had to throw it all away. And for the first week, that's pretty much what we did."

The real struggle began after the trash was gone. "We have no business anymore," he said. "What do we do? Where do we find money? Who do you go to? How do you help your staff? How do you tell people what's going on?"

They set up a game plan, just to keep the momentum going as best they could. There was a physical plan, a financial plan, and a marketing plan to attempt to communicate with the public.

Photo: Woodstock Farmer's Market

This is what the sales floor looked like, with displays tipped over and gooey mud covering the floor.

Photo: Woodstock Farmer's Market

Employees and volunteers take on the daunting task of cleaning up the market so it could reopen.

"When the wheels fall off, the wheels fall off. And on the 28th of August, we had a business. It was a full machine, moving down the street. And on the 29th, we had nothing. And then there were all the bills. A lot of bills. And they needed to get paid."

They set to work on their website, sending out e-mails and posting updates on Facebook. They devised the Irene Card, a prepaid shopping card that allowed people to give money up front and shop when the Market was back on its feet. And while all the hardline problems of relaunching a business are daunting, the emotional toll took its own brutal course. In a blog post from their website during this time, Amelia, one of the employees putting the business back together, wrote:

"We are people who love what we do. When we lost our outlet for expressing that love, we experienced profound feelings of grief and loss and have had to come to grips with our compulsion to express ourselves in other ways. Lisa has cleaned her garage and is frantically pickling and preserving fall produce. Abby is comforting herself with daily Nutella sandwiches. Steve P. continues to put in 8 to 10 hours a day in the office on the computer. I listen to hours of books on tape. We each have our way of ignoring reality."

Months later, the store is up and running with few signs of the flood except for the photos posted on a back wall. Looking back, Crowl said, "Probably we all need grief counseling now. Everyone is still struggling with various and sundry parts of such a big loss."

In the days following the initial damage, he recalled how thankful they were to have such incredible help and support

Photo: Woodstock Farmer's Market

A volunteer performs the "dumpster toss."

from the community. The pictures show the wreckage but also the family, friends, and staff covered in mud—but still smiling.

"Woodstock's a great community, and that's what makes it a great place to live," he said. And it's a community, truly a community, and it's got very strong roots. When you're a real part of the community, people don't disappoint you by not supporting you. There was a very large contingent of people who helped—even the people who weren't here wrote to us and donated to us, gave us loans. We had a lot of good support."

Amelia wrote on the store's web page, "There have been many beautiful moments for us in the weeks since Tropical Storm Irene raged through our store. The love and sympathy and support from our loyal shoppers has been a tsunami, dwarfing the flood that we experienced in comparison."

Just a few yards down the street from the market was the office of the *Vermont Standard*, the oldest weekly newspaper in Vermont, which was inundated by the same flood that ran through the market, four and a half feet high, drowning desks, equipment, files and the eleven computers that employees used to get the paper out every week.

Photo: Vermont Standard

Philip Camp, right, publisher of the Vermont Standard, **in front of the newspaper's demolished office after the storm.**

In the midst of the most important local-news story of the century, there seemed to be no way the paper could print an edition that week. It turned out, however, that Irene was no match for Phil Camp, the native Vermonter and local skiing expert who bought the newspaper in 1980 and now serves as its publisher.

"The paper is 158 years old," Camp said, "and in all that time

Photo: Vermont Standard

Inside the Vermont Standard's *newsroom after the flood.*

it never missed an issue. I didn't want to be the one yo break that long tradition."

News was happening everywhere. Route 4 had collapsed in dozens of places, the historic Quechee Covered Bridge had been ruined, residents were being rescued from their flooded houses, a mobile home park across the river was full of ruined trailers, and cars and trucks were being pulled downstream in the flood. But how do you report the news with no electricity, no phone lines, no computers, no office and no way to get your reporters to the scene of the story?

"When I got there in the early afternoon on Sunday I drove the delivery van to my brother's house (to keep it from floating away.) I wasn't gone more than six or eight minutes, but by then it was clear we would have to leave. It was a metal building and you could hear it move, straining against the water. At that point it was literally a matter of saving our lives. There was no way we could salvage anything. All my personal memorabilia from my years in the ski business and the newspaper business all floated down the river."

Luckily there was a brand-new office building just down the road, but on higher ground. Camp quickly acquired it, but it was just an empty office with no furniture, no computers, no phones and no files. Camp bought some picnic tables so his staff had places to work dressed in their overalls and mud boots, but it quickly became evident that what they really needed were the files from the old computers, the ones now covered with inches of mud in the old building.

A local computer repairman said that if they could somehow salvage the ruined computers, he might be able to remove the hard drives and rescue the information on them.

"So we went back into the old building and dug out all eleven computers and by Thursday morning (four days after the flood) we were up and running. Suddenly it became possible that we would actually publish that week. It was crazy but at the same time it was exciting, even miraculous."

The *Standard's* web page stayed up throughout the flood because it was being run by the webmaster in Charlestown, New Hampshire, and news was flowing in from all over, stories, photos and videos that were all posted online in real time. The

Photo: Vermont Standard

Salvaging what was left of the newsroom after the flood.

scenic and historic Quechee Covered Bridge was damaged at both ends and the Taftsville Covered Bridge had also been damaged. Many communities became islands when roads and bridges collapsed and there was no way to get in or out. The website included vital information on where to seek help. Over 2,000 photos were collected that week.

The reporters and photographers used cell phones instead of landlines, and drove all-terrain vehicles to the isolated news sites. Pictures, stories and video footage began coming in from all corners of their circulation area; and they posted them on the *Standard*'s web page, which became an important clearinghouse for flood information at a critical time. It was on the website at 3:45 p.m. on August 28 that Camp made his now famous rallying cry:

"For 158 years the *Vermont Standard* has never missed publishing an issue, despite fires, floods and other disasters. We want to assure our readers that this week will be no different."

It seemed an impossible goal, but just five days later, on September 2, the presses in White River Junction began to roll at 4:30 p.m. The paper hit the streets a few hours later and was delivered to shops and subscribers throughout the region. In

The front page of the Standard's *Sept. 2 issue.*

some cases the individual papers could not be home-delivered because the roads were washed out, but they were picked up at post offices and general stores. The *Standard* printed 500 extra copies and many residents took more than one, knowing it would be a perfect souvenir of that historic week.

The one thing that was missing were the labels that go on the individual papers. They were lost in the flood and could not be replaced, but the local post offices allowed everyone to pick one up on the honor system. "We found ways to deliver to every one of our sixty outlets," Camp said. "In some cases we had to go through back yards and fields to get there."

Downriver in Quechee, home of one of Vermont's major tourist attractions, Quechee Gorge, the Ottauquechee River, which had formed the gorge many centuries ago, had turned into a destroyer, tearing down historic covered bridges and washing cars and trucks into the raging torrent. Among the debris were parts of houses, entire golf course bridges and white propane tanks, which were caught in the falls underneath the 80-year-old Quechee Covered Bridge. While some of the tank valves were closed, others were hissing with the sound of leaking gas, so town manager Hunter Rosenburg ordered an evacuation of the area, fearing that the tanks might cause a fire or even an explosion.

Eventually the relentless pressure from the raging river washed away the bridge approaches on both sides and the real estate office on the village side was gutted. The bridge itself survived, but it was no longer connected to the roadway on either side. The town waterline that used to run under the bridge, carrying drinking water to the lower part of town, was severed and caused water faucets to stop running.

The ground floor of the Simon Pearce glassblowing studio, just upriver from the bridge, began to fill with river water, and the adjoining restaurant, with its scenic view of the river, was now hanging over the edge; many feared it might fall in as the shoreline eroded in the flood. The Lakeland Golf Course was flooded and Alex Adler's house and his Parker House Inn were both damaged. The quaint part of Quechee was cut off from the rest of town, forcing customers to drive several miles to get there. The loss of the bridge cut the village in half, with people

Photo: Wendell Davis (FEMA)
The historic Quechee Covered Bridge, the heart of the town. Residents cried when they watched their beloved bridge battered by trees and debris on August 28. The girder at the left was put in place after the flood to hold the water line under it.

on one side only rarely in touch with those on the other side.

Eventually the water line was restored via a girder that was attached to the bridge and the shore, creating a support for the pipe, but over the winter, Quechee residents debated what to do about the bridge. All of the options were expensive at a time when town residents were struggling with repairing their own homes and businesses.

The town of Hartford, in which Quechee is located, put up a $1 million local bond for citizens to approve; it would be matched with federal funds to build a new bridge that would have a concrete foundation instead of the old wooden one, but would still be a "covered bridge" because the cover would be made of wood. Some town residents said they would rather repair the old bridge to make it the same as it used to be, which was estimated to cost $170,000, all of it paid for locally. If the bond issue fails, that will be the only option left.

Construction is already underway to repair the Taftsville Covered Bridge, just upriver from the Quechee Bridge, using $3 million in federal, state and local funds.

The water taps in Woodstock were still not flowing on Thursday after the flood, making it difficult for residents to clean up the mess. Many of the historic homes on Elm Street, Maple Street and River Street were flooded. The Woodstock Inn and Resort in the middle of town was closed due to flooding. At the Riverside Mobile Home Park, across the river from the *Vermont Standard* and the Woodstock Farmer's Market, house trailers were washed off their concrete slabs and swept down the river. Dozens of residents lost their homes and were forced to stay with friends and relatives.

With electrical power and cell phone towers out, many residents were tossed back a century to an era of kerosene lanterns and candlelight. Tom Morse, a selectman in the town of Barnard, recorded 9.5 inches of rain on his home gauge. One of the essential ingredients for the recovery, he said, was a steady supply of gravel, which was much in demand as the summer turned into autumn. In some places in Vermont it was brought in by railroad car to fill the huge holes in the highway that Irene had washed away.

On the northern edge of Barnard, Route 107 was one of the most damaged highways in the state. Gaysville and other towns

Photo: Craig Brandon

The Taftsville Bridge was also damaged in the flood.

Photo: Vermont Standard

A truck caught in the river is tied off until it can be hauled onto dry land.

along the White River could be reached only by ATV over old mountain roads. State Police Sgt. Barbara Zonay told reporter Sara Widness of the *Vermont Standard* that she was standing at Toziers Restaurant and looking out at where Route 107 used to be. "It looks like there was never even a road there," she said. "It's that extensive. I've never seen anything like it. The river just came in and took the whole thing away." Helicopters dropped cases of bottled water and military MREs (meals ready to eat) into the isolated communities.

In West Windsor, the firehouse was filled with three feet of water and some firemen were nearly trapped inside as the current ripped up the pavement outside and sent it down Mill Brook. The scenic covered bridge on Bible Hill Road near Route 44 was torn loose from its foundation and floated down the river until it ended up in a nearby field

Jeff Tucker, 17, of Woodstock rescued three drivers from swamped cars in front of his house at the corner of North and River Streets. The cars, one after another, drove into the high water and got stuck when their engines stalled. Jeff put on a life jacket and tied a rope around himself and headed toward the first car, which was caught in the current of the river and began floating away. "The water was up to my shoulder," he told the *Vermont Standard.* "I reached for her hand and missed her hand." The car started to float away but Tucker finally managed to grab the driver and pull her to safety. After rescuing Kate McClintic, he reached the other two cars and rescued Nan Bourne and Beryl Spencer, who were floating in a car with Nan's dog, Molly. The three women had been ordered by police to evacuate their homes on River Street and were headed for a shelter at the Woodstock Inn. "It just didn't seem that deep," said Spencer of her ordeal.

The towns of Mendon and Killington became islands when sections of Route 4 washed away and bridges collapsed. Tourists were trapped for days at the Killington Ski Resort; one chose to charter his own helicopter, which landed nearby and returned him to the outside world.

Further upstream on Route 4 in Bridgewater Corners, the Long Trail Brewery is equal parts Vermont craft brewery, local hangout, and tourist attraction. A world map on the wall is scattered with pins representing visitors from every time zone, and the bar stool next to you is just as likely to belong to a brewer

Photo: Nancy Nutlie-McEnemy

The Bible Hill Road Covered Bridge in West Windsor after it floated down the river and ended in a field.

Photo: Nancy Nutlie-McEnemy

A bulldozer clears debris from a riverbed.

living just over the mountain as it is to a beer-loving traveler dropping in for fresh, local food and drink. But on the morning of August 29, this welcoming space put on another hat, opening its doors as a community hub with the distinctive Vermont resilience that would become all too familiar as the state rebuilt, amazing the country and Vermonters too again and again over the course of the coming weeks.

The brewery was damaged, but it was minimal in comparison to the surrounding community. When workers arrived they were greeted by mud. Massive quantities of dirt and silt were mounded around the building to the point that they couldn't get inside. Garrett Mead, the Long Trail Visitors' Center manager, recalled confusion and devastation everywhere.

"The entire area was an island, even the post office was almost washed out," he said.

The brewery team removed the conference table from the office and carried it out into the driveway, and began the process of feeding both the local community and the volunteers working to muck out the mess. The brewery provided meals throughout the day for families, displaced kids, and workers fresh off the roads and bridges. It became the home base for Central Vermont Public Service workers who were working to get the lights back on.

"We kept the guys fed all week long, and the only thing we didn't give away was beer, because we weren't allowed to," Mead said.

It was hot that week, and they brought out ice pops for the kids. Garrett recalled two little girls who came to get them. They were excited about more than frozen treats though. They had just found their toys, safe in their bedrooms. Unfortunately, their house was only being kept from floating downstream because it was pinned—in the water—against the Hail Hollow Bridge.

If volunteers came, Long Trail fed them, too, preparing 150 box lunches at a time. They came from dozens of states and towns,

Photo: Nancy Nutlie-McEnemy

Construction crews helping to clear the roads and rebuild the roadbed after extensive erosion caused by Irene.

Photo: Audrey Richardson, Vermont Standard

Cadets from West Point, including two from Hartland, helped rescue the Barron Hill culvert pipes after they floated down Babcock Brook.

ringing tools, trucks, and anything else that could possibly help. Long Trail was a place where they could rest, unwind, exchange stories, and recharge.

One of the volunteers, a man from Iowa, was put to work out on the roads, directing traffic. As he put in his shift under the perfectly warm, sunny skies of early September that followed Irene, a local woman came out to see if she could offer him anything, maybe a drink. He was blown away, saying, "How can you possibly come out and try to help me? You just lost everything, everything you have." She responded simply, "Well, I've got water."

More and more stories of local heroes trickled in. Rob Campostella, a landscaper, took his excavator out while the storm was still raging to save a bridge. Jim Earle and Mike Olmsted fought to open an old logging road so people could finally travel north and south to Ludlow. Jeff Bridge left his heavy equipment in the parking lot for anyone who needed it.

The brewery became a makeshift helipad, taking supplies by

helicopter to Rochester, Bethel, Pittsfield, and other neighboring towns that had become islands overnight.

"I was staying with friends in Pittsfield. They told me I couldn't get home. So I said, okay. And I grabbed my backpack. And I hiked." This is how Jessica Johnson's story begins.

Johnson works at Shackleton Thomas, workshops and studios that produce handmade furniture, woodworking, and pottery in the finest artisan traditions. Approaching Shackleton

Photo: Phil Camp, Vermont Standard

A crane pulls a damaged truck from the river.

Thomas from Route 4 only five months later, it would be hard to imagine that most of their workspaces were entirely covered by Irene's water and sludge on August 29. An unassuming dirt road leads off the highway past pottery studios to a generous parking lot outside the converted mill that houses not only the Shackleton Thomas artisans, but also a whole community of artists and crafters from weavers to hair stylists. There's a bar and restaurant, as well as the Bridgewater Post Office.

Inside the mill, the lovingly renovated showroom houses hand-carved cheese boards, warm hardwood furniture, in addition to shelves of elegant pottery of all shapes and sizes. It's a dream for those who love or collect purely crafted work for their homes.

"It's easy for people to come in here and complain about our driveway," said Johnson. "They don't realize that it used to be a hole. A giant hole, in the ground."

Upon arriving at the Shackleton Thomas showroom and asking about the storm or complaining about the parking lot (whichever comes first), Johnson takes guests through the showroom toward the entry to the workshops, buzzing with

Photo: Angela Drexel (FEMA)

Mud, rocks and debris had to be cleared from many streams and rivers.

Photo: Wendell Davis (FEMA)
Workers repair a damaged bridge.

the sounds of heavy wood being carried and saws humming. Located on the level below the showroom, all the precious local hardwood is stored before it is readied for generations of families to dine upon or crafted into a fine side table. It's also the home of tools and workspace for many talented craftspeople.

Wide stairs lead down to the workshop's entry doors. Curiously, in a space of mostly neutral colors, the walls around the stairs are painted bright blue nearly to the top.

"So that blue is the waterline; Charlie Shackleton came in and painted it to remember. It was eight feet or so."

In a post on the Shackleton Thomas blog, the retail manager painted an even more vivid picture:

"We woke up Monday morning to a deceptively normal ,bright sunny day. The news reports on Vermont Public Radio that morning were not so bright: roads washed out, bridges collapsing and floating away, houses destroyed and lives lost. It was surreal. So surreal. Even as I went for a jog along my regular running route alongside a (now very much wider) brook, I glanced into the normally clear open field and it was covered with sand and rocks. And then on second glance, oh my

Photo: Wendell Davis (FEMA)

Bowers Bridge in West Windsor is one of two tied-arch design bridges in Vermont. Irene washed it 200 yards down the river. Workers are restoring the bridge and moving it back to its original location.

goodness, there's a covered bridge in the field! It would normally stand so strong and tall spanning the bridge over Mill Brook, but it was swept completely off its foundation and is now the primary (dare I say decorative) feature in the field. The lawn adjacent is filled with sofas, mattresses, duvets and other household goods now desperately trying to dry out in the sun before mold sets in. Oh dear—what a mess. Reality is still setting in. I could only begin to imagine the volume of water that gushed so rapidly, filling our basement with eight feet of water. It looked like a hurricane had hit."

Johnson said they had to shovel out mud just to open the doors to the workshops; the walls had been ruined by water and mud, requiring new sheetrock. The process of clearing out the space had everyone in muck boots, hauling out sodden lumber piece by piece. Fortunately, with a great deal of manpower, they were able to clean it off and dry the bulk of the wood in a borrowed kiln, rescuing the material for use in future work.

"It was amazing that we could save it—it was worth thousands and thousands of dollars, and we can actually use it. Even after all that muck."

The machinery was not so lucky, and many motors and parts had to be replaced, including Miranda Thomas's much loved kilns, which had been a fixture in the pottery studio for 15 years. The studio, while housed in a separate building, sustained significant damage of its own.

"It was a process of sorting through stuff, just stuff, knee deep, to see what we could find," she said. "We had a ton of community support. People were really great—we set up everything in the parking lot and just shut down. Over the course of a month we cleaned and rebuilt. We were still open online, doing orders with what we had in muck boots and headlamps. We had a crazy sale on pottery—people were amazingly supportive. But it's not something that happens overnight."

The pottery sale focused on a small quantity of pots that had been rescued from the waterlogged studio and were sold to help with Irene damage. Online fans snapped them up in hours.

Photo: Robert Rose (FEMA)

A car was stranded when a section of Route 103 in Ludlow collapsed after flash flooding caused by Irene.

Photo: Wendell Davis (FEMA)

Irene's torrential rains caused roads to crumble as floodwater undermined highways such as Route 4 in Killington.

"All I could picture while I was at home during the storm was pots, just bobbing down the river," Johnson said.

Much to their relief, the potbobbing never happened in the Ottauquechee; the new showroom and the goods housed there made it through Irene unscathed. But the space is far from untouched; aside from pictures lining the blue-painted stairwell, a slideshow display slowly rotates images recording the damage and cleanup adventure of this small team, and the weeks in muck boots that changed their business forever.

Only the folks at Shackleton Thomas, and perhaps the most discerning collector, would notice another subtle difference in the showroom. Throughout shelves and displays of elegantly patterned black-carved pottery, a few pieces stick out. They were the first to be fired in the new kilns, exciting replacements for the trusted equipment claimed by Irene. It was tough, Johnson mentioned, to figure out the new equipment at first. There were things to learn and kinks to figure out, in the same way as one must when working with a new person on staff or getting adjusted to a new house. In this case, the pots came out with a slightly different hue—the glaze came out foggy, with bluish and greenish tints instead of the trademark rust color that the artists sought. Though this problem was easy to solve, especially compared to the struggle of previous months, there's a certain poetic quality to those first few new pots to emerge after the flood—just a bit cloudy, and just a bit blue.

Shackleton Thomas was far from the only one touched; throughout the mill, the resident artisans all show these small changes, and all have their own stories. Karen Hartland, one of the weavers who works in an upstairs studio, recalls walking through the street after Irene and meeting a woman who was just handing out shrimp scampi, trying to feed people before the food spoiled. Months later, the two are now friends who make plans to meet for dinner. Chris Navus, the bartender at the Ramunto's pizzeria downstairs, still marvels at how much water was in the building. "Eight feet of water under these floor boards. There was eight feet!"

Navus' house, just off of Route 4 near Mendon, had its own set of problems during the storm. Houses, driveways, and even roads to access the much-damaged Route 4 were washed out.

Photo: Wendell Davis (FEMA)

More road crumbling in Killington.

He remembers the sheer craziness at the height of the flooding—water rushed all around his and his neighbors' property, cutting garages in half and overwhelming driveways.

Originally from Long Island, Vavus had been preparing to shelter people. "I called my family and everybody in New York, and I'm like hey, come on up to the mountains, guys, we've got guns and food, and you know, it's Vermont." When the tables turned and he found himself with the storm damage predicted for his family in the city, Chris was unfazed. After all, this is Vermont.

Through an incredible effort from volunteers, road crews, and the very Vermonters Navus was talking about, Route 4 reopened just 19 days after Irene took it out. It may not have been pretty, and there may have still been quite a lot of work left to do, but it opened nonetheless. When Vermont Public Radio broke the news of the statewide celebration of this achievement, they tallied up some of the damage that had been heroically repaired in just under three weeks:

Route 4 between Rutland and Bridgewater was damaged in several locations, including five places between Mendon and Killington where flooding from Mendon Brook created major roadway craters. In two locations, all three lanes of Route 4 were missing. In other locations, two lanes were missing with sheer slope drops of 70 to 80 feet.

Portions of the roadway were also completely washed away in Killington around River Road, and there was damage in several other locations along "Killington Flats" and the rest of Route 4 stretching east to Woodstock.

As Rachel Maddow said when she showed the infamous Route 4 video on her MSNBC broadcast, "You say problem. Vermonters say challenge."

"You can see that this community is coming back," said Phil Camp. "We lost the leaf-peeping season, but people made the most of it. Tourists weren't taking pictures of the leaves anyway; they were photographing the upside down cars in the rivers or bulldozers rebuilding the roads.

"I've lived here all my life and there are all kinds of people in our area, rich and poor. You would never expect someone who has maids and butlers to put on their barn boots and go out

Photo: Nancy Nutlie-McEnemy

Flood damage on Route 131 in Amsden, Vermont.

and help muck out a neighbor's home. I'm a Vermonter and the spirit of being a Vermonter was never clearer to me than it was then." ✍

Photo: Weston Playhouse

The remains of the baby grand piano that once graced the orchestra pit at the Weston Playhouse Theater.

Irene was no connoisseur of the arts

The Weston Playhouse Theater in the quaint little central Vermont town of Weston was four performances into the world premiere of the play "Saint Ex" by Sean Berry and Jenny Giering, about the life of the famous author and aviator Antoine de Saint-Exupery, when Irene forced the theater to go dark on August 28.

The West River, which normally creates a pleasant overlook from the back porch of the white colonial theater building, covered the grounds and filled the basement up to the ceiling. While the lobby, auditorium and stage weren't damaged, the orchestra pit, basement and sub-basement were destroyed, including a part of the basement that had recently been renovated.

The theater lost its extensive collection of 1940s costumes used in the play, including wigs, hats, dresses, leather flying jackets and helmets. Its costume-making shop, dressing rooms and laundry rooms were a total loss, but the orchestra pit took the hardest hit. Recently rewired for optimal sound, the wiring was gone and the Baldwin baby grand piano that was the centerpiece was found upside down, its keyboard frozen. Drumsticks were floating in the water.

When the water began to recede, all those shoes, hats and racks of costumes were laid out on the town green across the street in the hope that they might dry out in the hot sunshine. The piano, wrapped in a blanket, warped as it dried out, its legs smeared with mud. The props and sets were dragged out as well.

The play, which had just received a favorable review in the *New York Times,* was forgotten for a time as crews and volunteers rushed to save the theater. All of the wet sheetrock and layers of mud had to be removed to prevent mold. When a few courageous cast members managed to say "the show must go on," they were scoffed at. How could you produce a play with no costumes, no orchestra and no sets?

Just a week after the flood, however, the cast was back onstage with a greatly modified version of the play with no sets, no props, no costumes and limited music from a five-person band instead of an orchestra. The show went on for eight more performances with the original actors doing their best to recreate what was lost. When the performance shut down, the entire basement and orchestra pit were ripped out down to the bare walls. Estimates of the cost to make repairs came in at $100,000 to $200,000. The playhouse was celebrating its 75th season. The piano alone would cost tens of thousands of dollars to replace. Coming to the theater's aid were friends in New York who organized a "NYC loves VT" fund raiser.

Saint Exupery might have understood the theater's defiance in the face of disaster. The author of *The Little Prince* and other books, he was an accomplished pilot who joined the Free French Air Force in North Africa, despite the fact that he was well above the maximum age for pilots. He disappeared over the Mediterranean on a reconnaissance mission in 1944, but pieces of his plane were later found.

The Weston Playhouse was not the only arts venue that Irene terrorized during her visit to New England. At Tanglewood in the Berkshires, the Boston Symphony Orchestra was forced to cancel its August 27 performance of Beethoven's Ninth Symphony, the first cancellation in the 75-year history of the arts

Photo: Weston Playhouse

The costumes, scenery and musical instruments were removed from the Weston Playhouse and spread on the green across the street.

Center. Performances at Jacob's Pillow Dance Center were also canceled.

In Williamstown, Massachusetts, the Williamstown Theater Festival's new storage space and scenery shop was flooded. The Hoosic River, which had already destroyed the Spruces Trailer Park, filled the Blackinton Mill building in North Adams with ten feet of muddy water. The costumes and sets that had been collected over half a century were destroyed, a total loss. Until 2011, the shop had been located in the Delftree building, a 19th century mill in North Adams, but heavy snow had caused the roof to collapse and it was declared unsafe for occupancy. During the summer the theater's carpenters had rebuilt the second building as a theatrical scene shop, with a new floor, a loading ramp and a new electrical system, all destroyed by Irene. The bill in Williamstown was set at $350,000. ∾

8
Schoharie, New York

Doomsday sirens and ghost houses haunt a ruined valley as volunteers work tirelessly to restore it.

It's an unusually warm January afternoon at the Loaves and Fishes Cafe, and two dozen Schoharie County Recovery volunteers are eating their lunch of soup, pasta, sandwiches and cans of soda. Their overalls and shoes are full of mud as they sit on folding chairs around the long wooden tables, adding new anecdotes to the epic that has dominated their lives for the past three months and counting: the damage caused by Tropical Storm Irene.

Using donated food that arrives nearly every day from restaurants, supermarkets, churches and individuals, the cafe's food is cooked by volunteers and serves trauma-stricken residents, professional and amateur volunteer workers, and even visiting state and national officials who stop by at what used to be a church fellowship hall for a progress report on the town's recovery. The hall has become the unofficial center of town because the town hall, along with all the other public buildings, is still closed. A van collects donations from as far away as the Capital Region, providing boxes of food, paper plates and lighting fixtures from a hotel in Schenectady. Nothing is turned away and a use is found for everything, including baseball equipment and Christmas decorations.

The volunteers, a motley crew of church-group members,

Photo: Schoharie Recovery

A view of the flooded Schoharie Valley from Vroman's Nose, showing the wide area that was impacted.

college students, government employees, union workers, corporate volunteers and individuals from as far away as Washington, DC, have accomplished a lot in four months, but they still have a long way to go. Of the 940 people who lived in the village before August 28, only 20 families have been able to return. Schoharie is still a ghost town, with its former residents living with friends and relatives until their houses can be decontaminated and repaired. The piles of debris that once lined every street in town are gone, as is the football-field-sized debris collection point in a vacant parking lot on Main Street that was once the Great American supermarket.

Many of the houses, ruined beyond any hope of repair, have been torn down and their foundations bulldozed into vacant lots. The power is back on, the streets have been repaired and the Schoharie Creek is back within its banks, but as any of the volunteers will tell you, Schoharie is far from normal. The official estimate is that the storm caused $27 million in damage in the small village.

Of the 19 businesses that line the west side of Main Street, only four were open that January day. The others, including the hardware store, the laundromat, two cafes, the Glass Bar, an insurance company, two law offices, a computer store, a beauty parlor and an abstract company were all closed, many with the walls torn out down to the studs, the windows covered up and the floors still dirty from the mud.

Most of the shops were entirely empty. The former hardware store has discolored paint cans stacked up and racks full of dirty plastic signs. The sign for the former Main Street Cafe, which used to hang outside, is stored in the back of the empty space. One bright spot is Stewart's, the town's gas station and convenience store, which was destroyed by the flood but torn down and rebuilt in just a few days on the old foundation. However, the area's only supermarket, the Grand Union in Middleburgh, was directly in the flood's path. Floodwaters ripped out a trash compactor in the rear of the building, creating a large hole that allowed the water to flow through the store, blasting out the plate glass windows in the front. The building was filled with several inches of mud and the contents were a total loss.

The residential section of Schoharie, full of century-old

Photo: Craig Brandon

Row of empty shops on Main Street in Schoharie.

Photo: Craig Brandon

A downtown Schoharie business that has been "mucked out" with the floor and sheetrock removed up to the flood level.

Photo: Craig Brandon

Interior of the former Main Street Cafe, Schoharie.

Photo: Craig Brandon

The owner of this Schoharie house, which was damaged in the flood, jacked it up and built a new first story underneath it.

Victorian mansions and newer raised-ranch style houses, seems at first glance to be returning to normal, but a closer look shows this is only a facade. Open the front doors and look inside, and the houses are only empty shells, torn down to the framing and subfloors with all the flooring, sheetrock and furniture removed and emitting a musty odor, the last remains of the toxic water that flooded them as high as ten feet on August 28.

"The houses may look normal during the day," said relief worker Joel Bramer of Middleburgh, "but at night there are nearly no lights on because so many of them are empty." In some houses the residents live on the undamaged upper floors while they work to repair the first floor.

The almost unbelievable statistic is that of the 290 properties in the village before August 28, a total of 274, or 94 percent, were damaged by Irene. Entire houses have been torn down using bulldozers, leaving piles of debris that were carted away. With the houses gone, giant holes that formerly served as cellars have taken their place. After the holes were filled in, all that remains are driveways leading to nothing but "ghost houses," as one resident called them. Many of these lots now sport white, square FEMA trailers, where residents currently live. Among the flooded buildings were the county jail, the town office, the village office, the fire department, and the four county office buildings, where many essential records were damaged and recovery professionals were brought in to restore them. The Schoharie library, which was filled with 26 inches of water, lost 25 percent of its books.

Residents are busy making repairs to their homes, trying to get them sealed before the snow flies and they welcome questions from visitors about the disaster, but after a few minutes it's not unusual that they begin to cry, explaining that they can't talk about it anymore because they have to get back to work.

Farming has been a major enterprise in the Schoharie Valley since before the Revolutionary War, but most of the local farmers lost their entire crops, their barns and even their animals, many of which drowned or floated away in the flood. Dairymen herded their cows to nearby hillsides, aware that their barns were in the flood path, but others, like the Van Aller farm on Clauverwie Road lost all their cows to the flood. The crops that were not damaged or washed away had to be destroyed because they were contaminated with toxic water. Farmers, unable to sell their corn for food or even animal feed were offering the ears to burn for fuel.

After the flood, volunteers helped farmers walk their fields to remove the debris that had washed downstream, including trees, farm equipment, swing sets, parts of demolished houses, tires, tractor trailers and hot tubs. Leland Neff, a Schoharie horse breeder, put up color posters all over several counties in search of 22 horses he lost in the flood, including stallions, mares and foals. The posters featured pictures of the horses and their names.

Harry Ioannou, owner of the 140-acre Pindar Farm on Route 30 in Middleburgh, lost 233 of his 250 chickens, and when the bales of hay soaked by Irene began to heat up in the September sunshine, he lost a barn because they burst into flames from fermentation. His crops of soybeans and corn had to be destroyed because they were too contaminated to sell. A few weeks later he became the county's only casualty of the flood in an accident while clearing flooded trees from his land.

The degree of devastation is well known to Josh DeBartolo, the volunteer coordinator for Schoharie Recovery and impromptu

Photo: Judith Grafe (FEMA)

Farmer Harry Ioannou lost his crops, equipment, chickens, and barn to the flooding from Tropical Store Irene. He managed to save his farm stand and some fruits and vegetables. but in February he lost his life in an accident.

spokesman for their work. A local from nearby Middleburgh, his previous experience volunteering in the South following Hurricane Katrina made him an expert when no one in Schoharie knew where to start with the cleanup. "As soon as this hit, I had a good idea of what needed to be done based on my time in New Orleans and I knew some of the right questions to ask the FEMA representatives."

He has examined the interiors of nearly every home in Schoharie, leading volunteers in removing mud and destroyed contents, tearing out waterlogged sheetrock with hammers and crowbars and helping to shore up damaged foundations.

After an hour describing the work his volunteers have been performing, he offers to take a visitor on a tour of the area, pointing out the high-water marks on brick chimneys ten feet above ground, the scattered FEMA trailers where houses used to sit and homes that have been left vacant for months. In some cases the owners seem to have left town for good.

Photo: Craig Brandon

Josh DeBartolo, volunteer coordinator for Schoharie Recovery, examines the foundation of a Schoharie house damaged by Irene.

"A place like this is probably going to be a total loss," DeBartolo said, pointing out one house and noting how the floor joists had separated from the flooring. Clothes could still be seen hanging in a closet inside and black mold spores had climbed up the sheetrock to the ceiling. "I wouldn't even let volunteers go into a place like this," he said. "It's too dangerous." So the house is likely to be demolished, pulled down by bulldozers, to become another ghost house with a driveway that goes nowhere.

Nearby are houses that seem solid, but their siding and insulation have been removed, exposing the new, white plastic house wrap. If they get inside these homes quickly, volunteers may only have to remove the walls up to the high water mark,

Photo: Elissa Jun (FEMA)

A Schoharie house and yard full of mud three days after Irene.
BELOW: Piles of mud-covered debris lined the streets of Schoharie
for weeks after the flood.

Photo: Elissa Jun (FEMA)

Photo: Elissa Jun (FEMA)

A Schoharie house is reflected in the pool of water Irene left in the front yard.

but if left too long, mold grows up the walls and even the ceilings have to be replaced. The majority of these houses will likely be repaired, DeBartolo said, and construction trucks are parked out in front of many of them. But it will take a very long time for the work to be done.

"From the beginning it was go where you can, do whatever you can but move as quickly as you can because the need was so great, " said DeBartolo. About 80 to 90 percent of the houses have been gutted, and the remaining 10 percent are people who left or people still waiting for insurance adjusters. While much of the "mucking out" and demolition of sheetrock and flooring has been done to stop the formation of mold, he said, the reconstruction will take a lot longer because there is a shortage of funding and skilled volunteer labor. Many home owners and small business owners have lost their jobs because of the flood, bringing additional challenges to financing rebuilding efforts.

"This is not something that is going to be solved immediately; it's going to take years," he said. "This would be a perfect place for someone who was looking to rebuild an entire community, for instance, someone interested in creating a demonstration project for a green community."

Another astounding statistic is that until farmer Harry Ioannou died in February, there were no fatalities during the flooding, although there were a few near misses. People got trapped in their cars and houses and had to be rescued by the fire department. People in isolated areas were stranded for days when roads and bridges collapsed.

Photo: Hans Pennick (FEMA)

A damaged house next to a stream on Mill Valley Road in Middleburgh has its porch held up by a board.

"One 70-year-old man in Middleburgh heard the siren go off but a tree had fallen across his driveway and he couldn't get out," DeBartolo said. "He tried cutting the tree with a chain saw so he could drive to safety, but after 15 or 20 minutes he decided to head back into his house to get out of the storm. He went down into his basement to move things upstairs, but that's when he got caught in the rising water. As water rose on both sides of the cellar door, he became trapped and tried to kick out a window. When that didn't work, and the water was now above his waist, he tried wedging something between the door and kicked at it so hard he dislocated his hip before the door finally opened. Just as he tried to escape, his belt loop got caught on a nail and the water rose above his head to the ceiling. He had to go underwater to unhook it and then swim up the stairs where the water was already rising. He grabbed his television so he'd be able to watch the news and went to the second floor where

Photo: Adam DuBrowa (FEMA)

The tools of the house mucker's trade, used for months as volunteers helped clean up Schoharie. Besides mops and brooms they also used sledge hammers and crowbars to remove sheetrock.

Photo: Adam DuBrowa (FEMA)
A half-ton pickup truck is buried up to the windows with debris in Middleburgh.

he stayed all night as the water rose six feet into his living room. The next day after the water receded, he went down into the basement and pulled out of the wall the nail that almost cost him his life. To this day he carries that nail around with him as a reminder."

Besides the physical work, the volunteers have to be amateur psychologists. Referring to the piles of discarded personal belongings outside the houses as "debris" is not sympathetic to home owners' losses as "these are their lives," DeBartolo said, "personal treasures and family heirlooms, pianos that have been in the family for generations." But the strict rule is that anything touched by the contaminated water has to be removed.

One 87-year-old Schoharie man who lived in the house he was born in, which dated back to the colonial period, was too emotionally invested in the house to allow it to be gutted. So when he planned to be out of town for a week and a half, his son and daughter-in-law came to DeBartolo with an idea. Was there any way the house could be gutted and put back together in that short amount of time? Was it too ambitious?

"Impossible is not a word we use around here anymore," said DeBartolo. "Within 15 minutes of his leaving town we had thirty volunteers ripping down the walls. At the end of the next day it was gutted. On Monday we brought in industrial dehumidifiers and fans to dry it out, and during the next week we studded out the walls, fixed the plumbing, had electricians tackle the wiring, had a team do mold abatement and hung all the insulation. Then we coordinated with a local labor union to sheetrock the walls and bring in their painters.

"Just as we were adding the finishing touches the homeowner arrived, put down his bags and took a look around and said 'I see you've painted the walls.' It was priceless. As everyone laughed I thought about how over 100 volunteers came together in that house, supported by dozens more behind the scenes and I thought together we will rebuild this county, one house at a time."

The next stop on DeBartolo's tour of the damaged area was at Karkerdorf Road in Central Bridge, where five houses stood on top of a fifty-foot bluff over the Schoharie Creek. From the front they looked a little worn, but it wasn't until you walked around to the back that you could see the damage. Four of the houses were obviously unstable and needed to be torn down while repairmen worked on the other one. When you stood on the bluff and looked down at the water, it was impossible to imagine that the Schoharie had risen all that way and still had enough force to do all that damage.

After that, DeBartolo took his visitor to a level piece of land on Junction Road in Esperance with a damaged shed that used to cover a picnic area and large concrete pads scattered about. On August 28 this spot had been a mobile home park with eleven trailers, but now it was just an empty lot. The ruined trailers had been hauled off for junk. Like many trailer parks in the Irene Zone, it had suffered total destruction. The stream was far off, beyond the horizon and residents had received enough warning to get out in time, but their homes were lost.

Photo: Craig Brandon

The rear of a house on Karkerdorf Road in Central Bridge. The Schoharie Creek is normally down a 50-foot cliff at the right, but on August 28 it climbed up with enough force to ruin this house. BELOW: More than a dozen houses on Priddle Road along the Schoharie in Esperance were swept away, leaving only a mailbox and rubble. The Schoharie Creek is in the background.

Photo: Adam Dubrowa FEMA

Photo: Adam Dubrowa FEMA

Residents of Priddle Road are joined by volunteers from Bathesda House as they raise the American flag over the ruins of their houses on September 26.

The last stop on the tour was Priddle Road in Esperance, a bucolic area that used to house twenty summer camps and permanent homes on the banks of the Schoharie. This area had flooded in the past and had a "doomsday siren" designed to warn residents when there was a problem with the Gilboa Dam. While all the residents got out in time, the entire area was under about fifty feet of water, submerging even two-story buildings and leaving little behind when the water receded. In January, the empty lots where homes once stood had been marked off by their owners, but all that was left were outboard motors, snowblowers and hulks of wrecked cars. DeBartolo said his crews helped tear down the remains of houses that had washed hundreds of feet downstream.

Jim O'Dell, who spent his summers in a camp on Priddle Road and used to go tubing down the Schoharie, said the emergency siren was tested every Wednesday. "The general rule was that once the siren went off you had 45 minutes to get out because the water from Gilboa was coming," he said. "I've been the carpenter along here for years now and I've done work for every one of the fifteen buildings that used to be here.

"The section of the creek along here is like a funnel," he said. "I would have loved to be on one of the hillsides across the creek taking footage when the flood hit, not that I would have wanted to see my camp washed away. Once you get past this spot, the sides narrow into a gorge and there is no place for the water to go."

That was one of the reasons Priddle Road was damaged so badly, he said. It wasn't just that there were no steep banks to hold the water back; the walls of the gorge caused the water to back up onto the Priddle area. "The power was just tremendous. There are boulders the size of houses that were moved and stacked up."

Just down the road from Priddle is the town of Burtonsville, where the wall of water destroyed houses on Island Street, on an island in the middle of the creek, and along Collier Road to the

Photo: Adam Dubrowa FEMA

A ruined house on Priddle Road.

west of the stream. Then it ran through a nature preserve at the downstream part of town.

Just upstream from Schoharie, Middleburgh is farther along in its recovery, even though it was closer to the creek. Mike Vilegi, owner of the Middleburgh Hardware Store, which dates back to 1888, is open for business again after spending 17-hour days clearing out ruined merchandise and three feet of toxic mud. Getting up and running, he said, was essential to helping his neighbors recover, since his store is the only hardware outlet for miles around. But hauling $150,000 worth of merchandise into a dumpster took loads of effort, and even now his peg board displays are beginning to rot from the water damage. His little drawers of screws and washers were full of mud. In the days after the flood, when his cash register was still not working, he allowed desperate residents to take what they needed, allowing them to pay him later.

During the storm, Middleburgh residents took refuge at the top of Cotton Hill Road, from which they could see the water filling the entire valley below them. They descended later to view the destruction downtown, where the Chinese restaurant had its furniture turned upside down and was full of mud. The

Photo: Craig Brandon

A condemned house on the Burtonsville Island.

Photo: Craig Brandon
A house on Collier Road, Burtonsville, along the Schoharie Creek.

front window of the auto parts store was broken out and the front of Four Star Realty had been pushed in by the force of the water. Propane tanks at Hubie's Restaurant were spewing gas.

Understandably, many Schoharie Valley residents have abandoned their homes to start over again somewhere else far from the shores of the Schoharie Creek. Houses once assessed at $100,000 or $150,000 were sold for $10,000 or even $7,000 as the owners cut their losses, taking their FEMA payments with them. Many houses are still abandoned and their owners cannot be located, so they stand there, with their front doors and garage doors open, their concrete foundations broken into pieces and the mold growing up the walls.

DeBartolo said about fifty houses in the Schoharie School District had either washed away or were torn down, taking these properties off the tax rolls. At a time when the county and towns need millions of dollars to rebuild, the tax base has taken a significant hit and many residents have already moved away.

In the days immediately after the flood, Schoharie Mayor John Borst said, many people were so upset they were ready to pack up and leave. He called it a "canyon of gloom," noting the many "for sale as is" signs, but since then, more residents have decided to stay. "It's the people who are important, not the buildings," he told the Cobleskill newspaper. "People who have decided to rebuild are an inspiration to those who are undecided. I think spirits are starting to rise. I'm asking people not to make any hasty decisions."

Tim Schroon, who lives on Sunset Drive, told the *Albany Times-Union* that his house, assessed at $65,000, would be sold for $30,000. He never even considered rebuilding, he said, "We're going to be somewhere high and dry. Every time it rains, my son thinks it's going to flood." Nearby, a house assessed at $95,000 was on the market for $15,000.

Unlike most towns in the Irene Zone, Schoharie actually had a flood evacuation plan, with round signs directing motorists to higher ground. Flood-warning sirens connected to the Gilboa Dam, some 20 miles upstream, were supposed to warn residents. The sirens went off on the afternoon of August 28, but by then most of the area was already flooded and residents panicked as the rumor spread that the Gilboa Dam had failed and burst. But escape routes are useless when trees fall across roads and bridges wash out; many residents found they could not get out.

When discussion turns to the Gilboa Dam, many residents express anger and voice versions of a commonly held conspiracy theory. Schoharie had been sacrificed to protect Albany and Schenectady downstream, and the flood had somehow been diverted into their town. Few offer detailed explanations about how this happened, and the owners of the dam have vehemently denied it, but for many survivors, the Gilboa conspiracy provides a scapegoat for the disaster.

Those who have spent time along the Schoharie know its bipolar personality. In the summer it's a scenic bucolic brook that tinkles over boulders, the perfect spot to go tubing or picnicking. But in the spring, when it carries the annual snowmelt down from the Catskills, it turns into the raging torrent that on April 5, 1987 tore down the bridge that carried the New York State Thruway over it, killing ten people.

But even those who had lived along the creek all their lives were not ready for what happened on August 28, 2011. During

Photo: Adam Pennick (FEMA)

The Gilboa Dam, undergoing repairs after Irene, was the topic of many conspiracy theories in the months after Irene, but authorities insisted that the dam had not failed during the storm.

the late morning, the creek began to rise, but that was expected anytime there was a significant rainfall like the eleven inches or so that Irene dumped on the area. This time, however, the creek didn't stop rising until it became an angry, toxic, chocolate-colored destroyer that crept into houses and wore away foundations.

Blenheim and Middleburgh were right on the creek, but the village of Schoharie was a half a mile away and was not expecting any problems until the water was in their basements. When the flood sirens went off at 1:45 p.m, some people understood what that meant, others did not. Some thought it was just a fire alarm and others thought it meant that the Gilboa Dam had burst and

17.6 billion gallons of water were headed straight for town.

In reality, the dam had not broken, but because of a power failure and a clogged censor, the Gilboa engineers had lost their ability to tell exactly what was going on with the dam, so they activated the doomsday siren as a precaution. The result, from Blenheim in the south to Esperance in the north was mass panic.

"People were jumping in other people's cars to get to higher ground," said Joel Bramer of Middleburgh, a recovery worker. "People were driving through town at top speed and yelling out the window, screaming 'the dam is broken.' "

Butch Allen, 55, a retired truck driver from Blenheim, told the *Albany Times Union* the sirens sounded "like something out of the *War of the Worlds*." He waded through waist-high water to get to higher ground and moved back into his home in a few days, but many of his neighbors are gone for good. "A lot of people are scared of going through this again."

The local police and county officials also relayed the false alarm that the dam had broken. The reverse 911 system was activated, telling everyone in town to evacuate immediately. While the message was not true, it certainly helped to get people out of town and probably saved some lives.

"I think the engineers panicked and let water go," said David McSweeney, owner of the Parrot House Inn in Schoharie. "They knew this rain was coming and they could have taken more precautions, and it's easy to be a Monday morning quarterback, but it will be interesting to see what comes from the towns that are suing the people who control the dam."

On Monday, as townspeople returned to their homes and businesses to survey the damage, a rumor circulated once again that the dam was about to break. A week later, after Tropical Storm Lee unleashed another torrent of water, there was another mass evacuation.

The hamlet of North Blenheim (population 330) on the upper section of the Schoharie Creek is internationally famous for just one thing: the longest covered bridge in the world. Built in 1855, it had survived dozens of Schoharie floods, but on August 28, after water was seen running through it, witnesses said it broke free and washed away, coming apart as it floated away in the flood, sending its ancient wooden timbers downstream where

Photo: Craig Brandon

Main Street in North Blenheim was still a disaster zone four months after Irene.

some local residents collected them as souvenirs. One piece has been colorfully painted and is now the official sign for the Loaves and Fishes Cafe at Schoharie Recovery. The bridge is depicted on the town's official seal, and residents are still trying to cope with the fact that it is gone.

"The loss of the bridge is very depressing," said Town Supervisor Bob Mann. "I think most people are rather numb about it. Some people cry when you bring it up. Some are so busy trying to straighten out their own affairs that they haven't reflected on it yet, and others are trying to rebuild it or create a new icon in its place. The bridge was really the centerpiece of our existence. It defined us."

During the height of the storm the water rose so quickly that Blenheim residents didn't have time to evacuate. Destroyed bridges meant the town was cut off from the world for nearly a week, and it was difficult to get food and water to residents. Mann complained that Blenheim seemed to have a lower priority than communities farther downstream. Of the twelve homes that

The North Blenheim Covered Bridge in its prime.

were substantially damaged in Blenheim, he said, he expected none would be rebuilt. Some residents are abandoning their damaged homes and moving away, leaving it to local officials to demolish them.

"I'm confident Blenheim will fully recover," Mann said. "Obviously it won't be easy. There will be difficulty finding money and resources, but we love this place and none of us will stop fighting to bring it back."

As an example of how a few feet of water over a few hours can change lives, consider the case of Leslie Price, the Schoharie village clerk. She owned beauty parlors in Schoharie and Middleburgh, a house in Schoharie, and worked in the village office, all of which were destroyed in the flood.

"By Monday morning the town was transformed," she said. "You couldn't drive down the street because the mud was so thick and the National Guard had the roads blocked. I had to park my car and walk."

The front door of her Schoharie business had been severely damaged so she walked around to the back door. "Chairs were flipped upside down, huge plants were gone, and the whole place was full of mud and muck. You don't know what to do. Your mind is frozen. It's like you gotta be kidding. How do you figure out how to deal with this stuff? Once you start ripping the

walls out, it's only then you see how bad the damage is." She
lost her credit card machines and her pedicure chairs and had
to bring in industrial dehumidifiers to dry out the building to
prevent mold and mildew.

A day later she found similar conditions at her Middleburgh
shop. The village offices where she worked were also destroyed
and full of water, but a computer expert was able to retrieve the

Photo: Leslie Price

*Inside one of Leslie Price's beauty shops. Computer equipment and
beauty equipment are full of mud after they were underwater.*

Photo: Craig Brandon

Leslie Price in her new home: a FEMA trailer.

town information from her destroyed computer's hard drive. When she went home she found her house full of mud, the windows broken and the back wall of the foundation separated from the rest of the house. The high-water mark on the first floor was seven and a half feet high, just six inches short of the ceiling. Two weeks later it was declared a total loss and torn down.

Price tells this entire tale bravely with little sign of emotion until it comes time to talk about her cat, Diego, who disappeared during the disaster and was never found. Many Schoharie cats managed to survive the disaster and were later rescued from the roofs of houses, in one case after climbing up the inside of the chimney as the water rose. Price hasn't yet given up hope that Diego might yet be found.

"The whole place smelled terrible," she said. "It was a one-story house and had a pool and a deck. I watched them pull it down on September 11. There was nothing salvaged. All the furniture and all the clothing was contaminated by the water. I offered to wash it, but they said that wasn't allowed."

She stayed with friends for a few weeks before she was given a FEMA trailer, which has been set up on the vacant lot where her house once stood. Four months after the disaster, she faces financial ruin. The FEMA money was barely enough to cover the

Photo: Craig Brandon

Despite the damage and ruin, Schoharie residents adopted a defiant attitude, as this Main Street sign shows.

cost of the demolition of her house and she still has a $70,000 mortgage to pay off for a house that no longer exists. Both of her businesses are closed, although she hopes to reopen the one in Schoharie soon. Meanwhile the six hairdressers who worked for her are unemployed, further adding to the economic devastation in the town.

Despite all that, she thinks the town will recover. "Sure a lot of people are leaving, but some see this as an opportunity. There's

Photo: Craig Brandon

The flag is at half staff at the site of the former Blenheim Covered Bridge, with the town of North Blenheim across the Schoharie in the background.

a house just down the street that used to be worth $250,000 and a guy bought it for $25,000 and he is just so excited. It's an opportunity for people who are just starting a family. It might take years, but people will come back and we'll fill up the schools again. In the long run, I think everything will work out."

David McSweeney, owner of the Parrot House Inn on Main Street in Schoharie, lives upstairs at the inn. "At 6 p.m. on the 28th there were about two feet of water in the street, and that wasn't too bad, but two hours later it was up to eight feet and it was flowing quite rapidly down the street. It got up to three feet high in the bar."

The next day, when he was told that the Gilboa Dam was

about to break, he headed out for higher ground. Then, when Hurricane Lee arrived the next week and the reverse 911 system warned that the town could be hit again, he once again abandoned the inn.

It took 20 to 25 people working around the clock for two days to clean out the mud from the hotel, built in 1776. McSweeney brought in a portable dryer, but he was lucky that the walls weren't sheetrock but plaster and wood, "built like a ship" that didn't absorb the water. In preparation for the storm, he moved his tables and chairs into the basement, which turned out to be a mistake when the basement flooded up to the ceiling. He had to replace his carpeting and his entire electrical system, and the basement was a total loss, but he said he was grateful to be up and running so quickly when most of the businesses in Schoharie weren't open four months later.

"This town will come back," he said confidently, even though from the front of his hotel he has a clear view of the closed businesses on Main Street. "This town had already been hit hard by the recession before the storms came. You're going to see new people coming in to replace the ones who left. Life is what you make of it. If you want to lay down and crawl away you can do that, but you can also pick yourself up and start over." ❧

Photo: Elissa Jun (FEMA)

Todd Van Aller, a Middleburgh, NY farmer, provides a tour of his Irene-damaged barn to a FEMA worker.

Farmers lose crops, barns, animals and soil to Irene

While the flooded towns and villages got all the media attention after Irene hit, farmers struggled with the loss of their crops, barns and animals, as well as long-term damage to their land. The floods either washed away the topsoil or covered it in debris, mud and silt.

The Schoharie Valley and the Deerfield Valley, both severely damaged by Irene, are among the most fertile and productive cropland in America, so their loss had an immediate impact on local food prices.

When the creeks and rivers overflowed, crops like corn and

pumpkins were either washed away or bent over from the weight of all that water, but even crops that survived were not fit for human consumption because they were contaminated with toxic water. The Food and Drug Administration's rule was that any crop that came in contact with the water had to be destroyed. That included truck farms on which tomatoes, green peppers and squash were nearly ripe. The University of Vermont Extension estimated losses in that state alone totaling two million dollars.

Ginger Nickerson of the University of Vermont's Center for Sustainable Agriculture wrote a report distributed to farmers which said, "As painful as it may be to do so, all crops with edible portions that have come in contact with floodwaters should be destroyed or discarded. Floodwaters are likely to contain contaminants. Microbial pathogens that could be in flood waters include bacteria, viruses and parasites."

Upstate New York farmers with Irene-damaged property gathered at a conference in Goshen, New York on September 8 to discuss their plight with farm service agencies and government officials. "We were dealt a severe blow by Irene," said state legislator Michael Pillmeier. "I know each one of you is drained emotionally, physically and financially, but, as always, we will get through this together."

Stephen Reiners, a professor of horticulture at Cornell, said 2011 was a difficult year for farmers even before Irene because it was so hot and dry. Irene floated away much of the year's pumpkin crop, he said, and farmers found their pumpkins lodged in trees high above their fields.

Many farmers lost livestock in the flood, including horses, chickens and cows that drowned or floated down the rivers. In farms near Rochester, Vermont, for example, farmers had to teach cows to swim through the rising waters to get them to safety. Missing bridges meant the animals were cut off from their feed. In Richmond, Vermont, farmer Christa Alexander found that lambs who had escaped their pens had found refuge on a piece of higher ground but were still chest-high in water. Four of them eventually drowned but a fifth was saved by a kayak rescue. While most of her piglets drowned, the older pigs found their way to higher ground.

Irene's floodwaters were full of all kinds of toxins, including fuel oil, sewage and pesticides, some of which ended up being plowed under. Farmers attempting to rid their land of the layers of toxic silt were reduced to scraping it up and hauling it away, a time-consuming and backbreaking process.

When the water receded from their farms on August 29, farmers were faced with a nightmare. The land that had been filled with everything from hay to corn to vegetables the day before was now full of debris that included parts of houses, giant boulders, propane tanks and giant trees. The first step was getting out the tractor to haul all that stuff off the fields. At the Williams Farm in Deerfield, Mass., heavy equipment was brought in to remove the tons of sand that Irene had deposited, at a cost of $375,000.

Rocks of various sizes also had to be removed and much of that work was done by hand. Then tons of damaged and contaminated crops had to be removed. So what do you do with hundreds of tons of contaminated corn? In Rochester, some farmers attempted to burn it. It wasn't fit for human consumption or even animal feed. Farmers in the Schoharie Valley were selling it at a loss for fuel to be burned as an energy source.

Getting rid of several inches of contaminated silt, the same mud that city dwellers were mucking out of their houses involved using tractors or payloaders to scrape it off and dump it into trucks to carry to the local landfill. The unusually warm winter, with little snow, allowed farmers to work all winter clearing off the muck in time for spring planting.

The Kingsbury Farm in Warren, Vermont, lost tens of thousands of dollars worth of tomatoes, celery, carrots squash, herbs and leeks when Irene caused the Mad River to overflow its banks and briefly cover the cropland up to four feet high. It also washed away some of the topsoil.

"The biggest issue for us is the loss of the soil and land," Aaron Locker, the farmer who leases the land, told the *Seven Days* newspaper. When the water rose on August 28, he opened the doors on the greenhouses, allowing the river water to flow through rather than destroy the buildings. The next day, however, the greenhouses were full of wasted food. In the fields, squash vines were tangled with irrigation hoses and mildew

Photo: Elissa Jun (FEMA)

New York Governor Andrew Cuomo (right) tours an Upstate New York farm damaged by Irene.

was beginning to form. He estimated his loss at $100,000.

John Sayles, the CEO of Vermont Foodbank, said the damage that Irene did to stream banks meant future erosion was possible and he put much of his initial energy into stabilizing them.

The hay crop took a beating from Irene as waters invaded barns and silos, tearing open the white plastic covering that protects it from moisture. Water not only ruins hay but also creates a fire hazard when the hay begins fermenting, creating heat. One farmer in Middleburgh, New York found this out the hard way when his barn burned down.

George Honigford of Hurricane Flats Farm in South Royalton, Vermont, lost onions, broccoli, corn and carrots and suffered damage to his greenhouses. He said that at the height of the storm the water was rising an inch per minute or five feet in just one hour.

Nicole Dehne, the certification administrator for Vermont Organic Farmers, said the state's organic farmers need not worry about losing their organic status because of the flood, despite all the toxic substances that Irene's waters carried. Instead, she said, it would be considered "unavoidable residual environmental contamination."

Farmers are likely to suffer Irene's consequences for years as they attempt to restore land that was damaged. The silty, Irene farmland is dry and crumbly, while the undamaged land is moist and dark, the kind that farmers like. After scraping off the silty layer, the land will likely require many applications of compost.

❧

9
Waterbury, Vermont

With 200 houses and downtown businesses flooded,
a loss of state jobs threatens a town's survival.

When the knock on the door came at about 8:30 p.m., Jason Dalley of Randall Street had been expecting it. For the last few hours he had been watching the Winooski River rise up to cover the field behind his house, about two football fields away from the river.

"That field floods four or five times a year," he said. "It's what happens when you live in a floodplain." He had been listening to the weather reports about Tropical Storm Irene and watching out the window as the water rose to his back steps. Then his neighbor yelled over to him that his propane tank was floating in the water.

"So I went out and disconnected that and then the fireman came and told us we had to leave," he said. "He gave us an hour, but I didn't wait that long."

So what do you pack at such a time? Clothing, an overnight bag, medicines, pillows and blankets, a few toys for the kids. When their bags were ready a half-hour later, Randall, his wife and two children filed into the family Tahoe, just in time to watch their other car, a Volvo, float down the street.

He dropped his family off at the elementary school, which had been set up as a refugee shelter, but remembered that he had left

Photo: Craig Brandon

Jason Dalley tells his story from the porch of his Randall Street home, which was damaged by Irene.

his dogs in the house. So he drove back to Randall Street, which was now full of water, and went upstairs for the dogs.

"When I came downstairs I literally had to swim out the front door," he said. "That's how high the water was."

The refugees at the elementary school shelter spent their time collecting news and rumors about what was happening to their town. Some talked about what they would cook for dinner when they got home. Others discussed whether or not they would have to buy a shop vacuum to remove the water.

"Nobody knew how bad it was going to be," said Dalley. "Everybody seemed to be in pretty good spirits about what was happening. No one was too distraught about it." Kids ran through the hallways while their parents sipped free coffee. Neighbors who had not talked all summer were catching up on what college their kids were attending and who had new grandchildren.

It wasn't until they returned to their homes on Tuesday that the full impact of the flood became apparent. Although firemen had warned them that it was going to be very bad and to prepare themselves, residents were horrified at what they saw. The outsides of the houses were still wet and coated with mud and there were still deep puddles in the yards. Their lawns were covered in dark mud and light-brown patches of silt and sand.

Inside, their furniture had been tossed around as if there had been a terrible brawl. Cabinets were tipped over and china had been smashed. The worst of it was the mud, two to six inches of deep, dark, pudding-like goo that smelled of fuel oil and raw sewage.

"Everything in the basement and everything on the first flood was gone," Dalley said. "My home office and 90 percent of the kids' toys were gone. The water had come up four or five feet on the first floor." Any hope of returning to his home was dashed that day and it would be six months before the Dalleys moved back home.

"We pumped out the basement, and there was an onslaught of volunteers," he said.

Both sides of Randall Street were filled with dumpsters for three weeks as volunteers set about removing all the damaged furniture, carpets, clothing and bedding.

Multiply Dalley's story by 200 and you have some idea of the multiple disasters that the small town of Waterbury, (pop. 4,900) faced in the autumn of 2011: serious damage to roads and bridges, businesses knocked out, municipal offices flooded and an insurmountable homeless problem.

"Some 220 of 600 properties in Waterbury were severely affected," said Town Clerk Carla Lawrence. "Homes, businesses, all of it. It's been so much that there are several organizations helping to bring it back—Rebuild Waterbury, focusing on fund raising and construction, and Revitalizing Waterbury, helping with the businesses."

Temporary shelters were set up, but most residents found places to stay with friends or relatives, some of them out of town. Some pitched tents in their yards or lived in campers in their driveways.

The makeshift armies of volunteers began with the terribly nasty job of removing all that mud, filling up buckets and pouring them into the red dumpsters that appeared along the damaged streets. But it soon became apparent that the mud was the easy part. The toxic water that had invaded the flooded houses had rotted the sheet rock covering the walls and black mold had already begun to grow. Soon the cleaning operation became a demolition project as volunteers used sledge hammers and crow bars to tear out all the sheet rock and the wet insulation behind it. This debris also went into the dumpsters, leaving behind the bare stud walls that resembled the skeleton of a house. Clothing, furniture and anything else touched by the water had to be tossed as well. The dumpsters filled with the kinds of items that make up a pieces of a lifetime: family heirlooms, children's toys, CD collections, television sets and musical instruments.

There was a lot of depression, but at least there was company. On their way out to the dumpsters, residents and volunteers chatted about the best techniques for demolishing sheetrock and speculated about who was going to pay for all of this. The state? FEMA? Some other federal agency? Or were they going to foot the massive cleanup bills themselves?

Even residents who had flood insurance, like Steve and Amy

Odefey who live in a 100-year-old house on Randall Street, found it did not cover their personal possessions and would only cover damage up to their home's highwater mark. Odefey said no contractors wanted to sheetrock only half a wall because it was too hard to match the new with the old, leaving an unsightly seam.

Dealing with miles of red tape, FEMA forms and insurance claims proved a daunting task for residents with their hands full making repairs. That's when ReBuild Waterbury came to the rescue.

Mame McKee, volunteer coordinator for ReBuild Waterbury, said in March that forty of the damaged houses had been repaired to the extent that they had working kitchens; they were still working on sixty other cases that needed repairs or ran out of money for repairs. About a third of the homeless are staying with relatives or a host family they did not know before Irene. The extent of the recovery owes a lot to the 1,400 volunteers who pitched in to help. Some seven to nine homes were demolished because they were damaged beyond repair, including foundation failures.

"There are four stages to recovery," she said. "Rescue, relief,

Photo: copyright 2011 Orin Langelle

A kitchen in Waterbury after the floodwaters receded.

recovery and rebuild. And right now we are very much in need of skilled people." While anyone can muck out a house and tear out the ruined sheetrock, she said, "the recovery has reached the level that we need licensed plumbers and electricians. The most expensive parts of a rebuild are bathrooms and kitchens, and many families simply do not have the money to pay for new kitchen cabinets."

In some cases survivors have returned to their damaged houses but are living on the second floor while the first floor is being repaired. Instead of a kitchen, they have a microwave oven and a hot plate. Families with children spent the winter in a construction zone keeping warm with a space heater.

ReBuild Waterbury has many roles in the recovery, including buying building materials in bulk, providing legal advice and reconstruction tips and dealing with Waterbury's massive housing crisis. Some ReBuild Waterbury volunteers have taken homeless families into their own homes. Like other places in the Irene Zone, mobile home parks took the hardest hit. At Whalley Park in Waterbury, forty trailers were destroyed and at Petterson Park in Duxbury, all nineteen trailers were flooded.

Photo: copyright 2011 Orin Langelle

Household possessions had to be tossed into dumpsters.

Photo: copyright 2011 Orin Langelle

Ladders were set up next to dumpsters so residents and volunteers could fill them.

The two flooded trailer parks can't be rebuilt because they no longer meet zoning regulations about what can be built on a flood plain. So part of the effort is to find a home for new parks, which will make up a considerable portion of Waterbury's affordable housing when the town finally recovers, McKee said.

While many residents have been able to repair their homes and move back, coordinators like Carla Lawrence said that six months after Irene, streets were still devastated, with some properties sitting completely empty. Besides Randall Street, the storm damaged houses on Elm Street, Batchelder Street and South Main Street. Occasionally, these empty properties have signs out front with good wishes or goodbyes to neighbors, indicating just how far away the previous inhabitants have gone. One home has a child's boat outside, ready and waiting for the water to come back.

Tom Vickery, the town assessor, estimated that the damage to homes and businesses, not counting the highway and bridge repairs, would be $9.7 million and that created a severe blow to the town's tax base just when money was needed for repairs. It also created a massive unemployment problem just when money

Contents of houses became debris, set out on the curb for removal.

was needed for repairs and building materials.

Skip Flanders, the village president of Waterbury, can point out the water lines in his own house. Inside, many of the renovations have been completed, but outside, the havoc wrought on his siding and foundation is clear, and work is still in progress.

After the floodwaters receded, downtown Waterbury was such a mess that the police closed Main Street to traffic allowing the debris to be removed with a bucket loader that drove down the street scooping up everything in its path. It also allowed town crews to patch up the sinkholes that had developed along Main Street. The new fire station, Flanders noted, was filled with three feet of water. Fortunately, they were able to salvage equipment and their upper story remained safe. That space ended up being used as a temporary command center for town and village government and coordinators like Lawrence.

"It was a pretty amazing effort," Lawrence said. "People came from all over the country to help. Some had connections to the town and some didn't. They just wanted to help. And there was a lot to do."

To complicate the situation, institutions that usually serve the community in times like these were equally hard hit. Flanders' church, located just off Main Street in Waterbury, had its basement flooded. This was the space that served as social hall and gathering place for church and community members, as well as Sunday School classrooms.

Much like the Randall Street homes, it had to be stripped down to the bare walls and repaired. Months later, work was still in progress, and the congregation still depends upon another local church for gathering space.

"It's going to be good," Flanders said of the renovated church, noting that the disaster had given them an opportunity to insulate and weatherproof the space more efficiently, improvements that would save the church a great deal in operating costs. "There's always some sort of silver lining."

Tom Stevens, the local state representative, wrote an iconic piece for the *Waterbury Record* that spread from blog to blog, across social media, and by word-of-mouth during the storm recovery.

"By noon," he wrote, "the mud was drying into dust and cars were kicking it up into clouds that found their way into our eyes, noses and mouths. Through Sunday, we sat glued to the radio, listening to the stellar work done by the crew at WDEV. For nearly 24 hours, they stayed on the air and took calls from

Photo: copyright 2011 Orin Langelle

A Waterbury survivor takes a break from cleaning to talk with a friend.

around the state, detailing the damage done by hours of incessant rain, 6 to 7 inches in some areas, 9 in others. Bill Shepeluk, our municipal manager, visited the studios of WDEV frequently and gave us progressively worse news.

"First the mobile homes in Whalley Park, then Randall Street, then South Main Street—while the immediate news detailed what was happening in Waterbury village, the story was not solely about the village. We heard from callers across the state, even from Boston, detailing damage no reporter could possibly know in real time.

"The fire department and police department did their duty, notifying people of evacuation notices and giving them the opportunity to leave in safety," he continued. "The Congregational Church opened its doors again, echoing its role in the 1927 flood, and nearly 40 survivors landed there. Thatcher Brook Primary School opened its doors as well, and offered electricity and sleeping pads. Bill Shepeluk, Alec Tuscany and Celia Clark (whose house was underwater) were everywhere, monitoring, managing and protecting.

"And when we cried at the sheer loss and the impact this flood has made on our friends and families, we had more than one shoulder to cry on," he wrote. "Still, for all the damage and for all the upheaval for our friends and neighbors, we fared better than many towns around the state. Waterbury, and Vermont, will rebuild, and we will survive. Please reach out and provide help when you are able. There will be many opportunities."

Hope Force International, a disaster relief organization that has assisted flood victims at disasters around the country, including Hurricane Katrina, arrived in Waterbury on September 1 and visited each of the 200 homes that were damaged. In their official report they delivered their bad news to the town leaders. Some 8 out of 10 residents couldn't afford to pay contractors to repair the damage and would need help or they would never recover.

The areas around Waterbury were also hit hard. Moretown was one of the Vermont communities that were turned into islands when Irene destroyed bridges on either side of town.

Photo: copyright 2011 Orin Langelle
When the mud began to dry, it turned into a toxic dust.

Photo: copyright 2011 Orin Langelle

Dumpsters became a common sight on Waterbury streets.

Nearly 20 town roads collapsed and the town offices were ruined. Sewage backed up into the elementary school.

"There are no words. It's just devastating and heart wrenching. It's awful," said State Representative Maxine Grad, who represents Moretown. "A friend told me she knows a woman who was swimming in her kitchen, pushing her refrigerator back up on Sunday. That's how high the water was."

Waterbury's main tourist attraction, the Ben and Jerry's Ice Cream Company Headquarters, was undamaged in the flood. Cabot Creamery, Green Mountain Coffee Roasters and Lake Champlain Chocolates also survived. But others were not so lucky. Snowfire Auto, Vermont Peanut Butter and Artisan Coffee and Tea were all out of business. The Perkins-Parker Funeral Home lost a new $73,000 hearse and a van.

American Flatbread, a Waitsfield pizzeria, was hit with seven feet of water, destroying the walls and floor. George Schenk, the owner, said 200 volunteers showed up to help him clean up the mess. "It's been an exceptional outpouring of support and it kind of humbles you," he said. "It reminds us that we don't live alone, as much as we might think about living in isolation." The volunteers, he said, saved him tens of thousands of dollars in damages.

Jeffrey Larkin, co-owner of Arvad's Grill and Pub on South Main Street, has been in the same building for 22 years and never saw a drop of water until Irene. He borrowed $100,000 from the Vermont Economic Development Authority to make the repairs and replace his ruined inventory and soon reopened for business.

The Alchemist Pub, located a few doors away in the worst-hit part of downtown Waterbury, was one of the businesses that did not make it. The owners, John and Jen Kimmich, were at home that Sunday night when a friend told them what was going on downtown. It turned out that the water was rising everywhere, flooding streets and bridges all around town. Despite Jen's misgivings, John knew that he needed to get to the pub.

"I tried to stop him. I had visions of him being washed away in a car. But of course he went, and he promised he wouldn't drive through anything flooded. And it was fine at that point on Route 100, everything was fine, but then he got into town, and sure enough the water was right up to the building."

He made his way into the pub, shut off the gas lines, and pushed through to the basement door where his office and the brewery operations were located.

Photo: Nicole Garman

A flood-damaged house undergoing repairs.

Photo:
Nicole Garman

Lines painted on the corner of this building on Elm Street show the maximum flood levels from Irene (bottom) and the higher level from the flood of 1927 (above).

"I went in and it was just unbelievable," he said. "I opened my basement door and it was just brown, muddy water. It was smooth, it looked like my floor continued out into the stairwell. I just shut the door and walked over to the bar, and poured a beer and just stood there. And I got about halfway through it and I could just hear the tanks, boom, boom, bumping up against the ceiling underneath me."

Every tank of beer, every wooden barrel, every piece of equipment, from fermenters to wrenches was submerged in the muddy water.

"Of course everything was in the basement," Jen recalled. "We had the full brewery, custom walk-in, tanks full of beer— almost $200,000 worth of beer was in the basement. It was a huge amount of beer, like three or four months worth of beer. John had some beer in oak barrels that he'd been aging for years, and all of it was gone—it was just crazy."

But their business was far more than beer—it was a busy, bustling restaurant as well as a brewery, and the heart and soul of that business were the food storage rooms and the refrigerators and freezers.

"We had the office down there with all of our computers, all our software, all our records, all the brewing recipes, all our food storage, all of our dry storage, another walk-in cooler with all of our food, you know, whole fish and chickens and just everything was there," Jen Kimmich said. "And then we also had our malt storage, and we would hold about $20,000 worth of malt at a time just to make the beer. So yeah, we had hundreds of thousands of dollars there." They shared the bad news with their customers on their website:

"Make no mistake about it, Waterbury was devastated," they wrote. "At one point in the middle of the night, pretty much half the town was under around 10 feet of raging, muddy water, with the river officially cresting at 20 feet. Not only was the basement completely full, but the dining room and kitchen were also about hip deep. A business can be rebuilt though; individual lives and homes are so much more difficult, and for this one building there are 50 homes throughout Waterbury that are worse off."

The next day they posted this:

"Six hours in a basement has a way of getting someone tired.

Randall Street was enough to bring a tear to your eye. Dumpsters, trucks, piles, high-pressure washers and, no exaggeration, easily 30 times more people than actually live there. Waterbury's pretty amazing! Main Street was a dustbowl of dried river mud and dump trucks, contractors and community food-stands with free dogs and burgers. Shout out to the Fire Department and Green Mountain Coffee."

"We spent three full days with about 25 volunteers, going through in muck boots, in shit, petroleum, just fetid mess, taking pictures of every single thing and documenting it. Because when we met with the insurance person, who was there right away, all they kept saying was document. Document everything, document everything in that basement. And we documented everything, everything," Kimmich recalled. It was just disgusting, dirty work; work that you never want to do."

The process took days, and they went through, piece by piece, cleaning out and taking stock. Every piece of the devastation was filed and recorded for insurance purposes.

They eventually received a settlement from their insurance company, but it was disappointing. The check was for $20.

"And that's what really gets me upset to this day, having the masks on, working, and just the health hazard and everything else," she said. "This stuff was disgusting: whole rotten fish, chicken, and it was worth thousands of dollars, and we're taking pictures of all this stuff. And it was hot out, and we're digging out everything, computers, whatever was there, taking pictures, hoping we could get some money for it," she said. "We didn't get anything. And that burns me. Because not only were we going in to this disgusting mess, but we were going through and picking everything out, and taking pictures of it and documenting it."

The Alchemist Pub has closed its doors and the owners have chosen instead to focus on their new cannery operation. The pub has been taken over by The Prohibition Pig, a new pub run by a friend and serving Alchemist beer.

The One Dance Studio, Artisan's Coffee, and Super Thin Saws were among the flooded businesses that managed to reopen. At Juniper's Fare, a local café, the owners returned to find that not only had their facility been ravaged but the Snowfire car dealership across the street had lost every one of its cars.

Photo: copyright 2011 Orin Langelle

As in other places in Vermont, Waterbury's roads were turned into rubble.

Juniper's Fare was swamped with three feet of water, more than enough to damage equipment, furniture, and supplies, not to mention the structure of the building itself. Run by a volunteer effort, they created a journal to log the outpouring of support

Photo: Craig Brandon

Irene survivor Nina Brennan in her new shop with the sign from the old one.

they received in both manpower and donations as they tackled the process of rebuilding. The volunteers preparing fresh food just months later shake their heads when they think of the clean-up process.

The small café triumphantly reopened its doors at the end of September and issued the following announcement:

"After many long hours of cleaning, scrubbing, shoveling, cutting, and rebuilding, we are open. Come on by and grab a sandwich. There are still a few things being done to finish up, but we are serving up food! Also, you want to come by because there is a new layout. Things will look a bit different at Juniper's Fare but the excellent food and wonderful smiles are the same."

Many Waterbury businesses that rented space from a landlord were more flexible and did not have to wait for repairs. They just moved to another location, sometimes one that a previous business tenant had abandoned. The Proud Flower florist shop, which used to be located on Main Street across from the state offices moved closer downtown to Elm Street, which runs between Main Street and Randall Street.

"It was simply incredible," Nina Brennan said as she sifted through her memories of Irene and the shop that once was. A picture of her and her neighbor Phyllis Barry using shovels to scrape the mud away from the entrance to her old store was taken by an Associated Press photographer and published all over the world.

She also posted updates on her blog to keep her customers informed, including this one, posted just two days after the storm:

"Well, dear friends and customers, never fear. Proud Flower will rebloom as Prouder Flower, but it might take a little time. Yes, our building was sizably damaged in the recent flood and we are presently closed and evaluating the situation to reopen ASAP. I can only say that I am overwhelmed and humbled by the love and support I have received during this disaster that has affected me, my business and so many people across our great state. We will persevere! Thank you all for your love! support! hugs! calls! well wishes! and HELP in the nastiest of conditions! Love and prayers to all! Now that I have power restored I will keep you posted."

But after working on the building for a time, her landlord decided that the mess was just too great to ever be fixed, so she went shopping for a new building. In an area where so many buildings had been damaged by Irene, it was not easy to find a suitable space and when she did, she had to wait for the owners to remove six feet of water and mud that covered the red and

Photo: Nicole Garman

The sign at the entrance to the state office complex. Somebody has added a plea to the state to return the workers to Waterbury.

white tiled floor and replace the walls, stained with water damage.

Memory Lane, the previous tenant, had been an independent scrapbooking store, but the damage from Irene was so immense that the shop had to close its doors for good. While the property owner was able to assist and handle repairs such as new walls and structural damage, Brennan had to rebuild every element of her business; with painting, sewing, cleaning, and in some cases acquiring entirely new equipment. The large cooler used for her flowers didn't fit through the hallways in her new space, and her storefront counter had to be moved in through a window that was, fortunately, being replaced as part of the flood repairs.

Proud Flower "rebloomed" on November 12, after several weeks of both emotional and physical intensity. Less than two weeks before the opening of her new doors, Brennan wrote:

"This week I am focusing on emptying the huge storage container I have parked next to my old shop at 128 South Main Street. The good news is, the unit was a fantastic idea for temporary storage. The bad news is everything stored in the unit has to be rewashed/wiped/brushed. The dust during the

Photo: Nicole Garman

Waterbury town President Skip Flanders, one of the leading advocates for returning the workers to Waterbury.

weeks that followed was everywhere, even when items were cleaned well initially, the flood dust in the air settled right back onto them! Ugh! However, my new space is brand-new and fresh and clean and lookin' good. Can't wait for you to see!'

Even months later, she has retained her deep optimism and inspiration, and her neighbors and fellow business owners echo her sentiments:

Photo: Craig Brandon

Painters help repair a state building in preparation for the return of state workers to Waterbury.

"People were just amazing," she said. "And not that I would want something like this to happen again, ever, because it's horrible, but I want to help. I want to be able to show up on a doorstep with a bucket. Because that's what people did; they just showed up with a bucket."

The biggest blow to Waterbury's economy, however, turned out to be the loss of the State Office Building complex on South Main Street, right in the same Winooski flood plain as Randall Street. The 1,500 employees worked in 49 brick buildings housing everything from Human Services and Administration to Environmental Conservation and Corrections. Irene flooded the ground floors and basements of all these buildings, destroying not only the offices but also the essential parts of the state's telephone, computer, electric and heating infrastructure, which were stored in the basements.

At the exact moment of Vermont's biggest disaster in a century, all 1,500 of these employees were unable to help until new emergency offices could be located for them. In the meantime, phones went unanswered, computer networks went dead, vital information went uncollected and the state's emergency command center, one of the most vital of state agencies after Irene, had to be moved to Burlington, away from the flood, putting it out of action at a crucial time.

At first, Waterbury expected this loss of offices, jobs, and friends would be temporary and that the complex would soon be renovated and reopened, but it turned out not to be so easy. While Waterbury and the state officials who live there insisted it was simply a matter of flood-proofing the buildings and reopening them, many state officials thought rebuilding on a floodplain was simply asking for a repeat of the disaster in the future.

President Flanders made the opposite argument. Irene had already torn his town apart and now the state wanted to remove its largest employer for good? Those 1500 employees were what kept many of Waterbury's businesses going.

"These people didn't live here, but they were part of the community," he said. "They filled prescriptions and ate lunch and shopped in our stores, they bought flowers or presents or ran errands, you know. And now they're just gone."

Albert Caron, owner of a Waterbury car repair business, told Vermont Public Radio that half his customers were state workers, and now that they are gone his business was idle, unable to find customers to replace them.

The fate of the state offices went undecided for months. A survey of state workers conducted by the State Employees Union found that the vast majority of them wanted to return to Waterbury from their temporary offices around the state. The ones who lived in Waterbury could walk to work every day and the far away offices meant they had to buy cars and spend time commuting.

Just before spring arrived, the state announced a compromise that would allow 900 state workers to eventually return to Waterbury in updated and flood-proofed buildings. The 200 Public Safety workers who had already returned to Waterbury would be joined by 700 from the Human Service Agency. The other employees would remain in other locations, including Montpelier.   ❧

Photo: Craig Brandon

The remains of the Bartonsville Covered Bridge, twisted and upside down, just down the Williams River from its former location.

Covered bridges no match for the fury of Irene

Perhaps Irene's cruelest blow was the one she struck against some of the region's oldest and most venerated landmarks: covered bridges that had withstood the hurricane of 1938 and the flood of 1927 only to submit to the tropical storm's fury. At least a dozen bridges were severely damaged and a few were total losses.

When the Bartonsville Covered Bridge in Rockingham, Vermont, crashed into the Williams River at the height of Irene's flash flood, it might have been a lonely casualty were it not for the work of Susan Hammond, a local resident and bridge lover. She happened to be right there with her video camera to capture the moment for posterity, complete with X-rated voice-over, and posted it on YouTube.

It was Irene's "shot heard round the world" as the video went viral and became the best known image of the disaster as hundreds of thousands of viewers watched the dark-brown bridge as it quivered, then shook and finally just let go into the raging torrent that the river had become. Its intact but twisted body ended up a half-mile downstream, just avoiding a double tragedy. Had it drifted a bit farther, it might have collided with another covered bridge, the Worral Bridge, which suffered enough damage that it will also have to be rebuilt. A third covered bridge, the Hall Bridge in nearby Saxtons River was also damaged and closed to traffic.

Local residents were in mourning for their much-loved covered bridges throughout the Irene Zone. Best known of these was the Blenheim Bridge in North Blenheim, New York, which, like the Bartonsville Bridge, was on the National Register of Historic Places. Unlike the Bartonsville Bridge, however, it was no longer being used for cars or pedestrians. Said to be the longest covered bridge in the world, its image was painted on every official Blenheim car and truck. Now the flag at its former site flies at half staff as a tribute. No one is even suggesting that the bridge might be replaced. Although it was Blenheim's claim to fame and its only tourist attraction, Blenheim residents are too busy picking up the pieces of their ruined town to worry about the bridge.

Few of the Irene Zone's covered bridges escaped undamaged. Two covered bridges over the flooded Ottauquechee River, the Quechee Bridge and the Taftsville Bridge were severely damaged. The latter is already being repaired, but the former, eroded on both sides and damaged in the middle, was the subject of an ongoing dispute in town. Should the bridge be replaced with a more durable covered bridge with a concrete deck or be rebuilt as a genuine all-wood, authentic covered bridge?

It turns out that covered bridges are more than quaint, antique curiosities. They are engineering marvels, elaborately designed to be held together with wooden trusses, often reinforced with two-inch-thick wooden pegs. The distinctive roofs were not meant to shelter pedestrians and horse-drawn wagons, but to protect their wooden trusses from the elements. Without the roofs, the trusses were vulnerable to aging and would not have survived a decade, much less the 156th birthday celebrated by the Blenheim Bridge or the 141st of the Bartonsville Bridge.

Pieces of the Blenheim bridge were collected all along the

Photo: Craig Brandon
The Worral Covered Bridge, just downstream from Bartonsville on the Williams River, remained standing but will have to be rebuilt.

course of the Schoharie Creek and kept as souvenirs. One piece became the sign at the Loaves and Fishes Cafe, set up for flood relief volunteers in Schoharie.

The skills needed to rebuild the bridges have been preserved by the kind of carpenters who build with a traditional post-and-beam mentality and use drills that twist from wrist power and not electricity. But rebuilding in the traditional way takes a lot of time and money. That is what the town of Rockingham intends to do with the Bartonsville Bridge, according to Susan Hammond, who led the campaign to rebuild it, perhaps using some of the original wood that lies on the bank downstream. It helps that the town had a $1 million insurance policy on the bridge.

Among the other covered bridges damaged by Irene were the Giorgetti Bridge in Pittsfield, Vermont, the Benedict Crossing Bridge in Arlington, Vt. and the West Arlington Covered Bridge over the Battenkill in Arlington, Vermont, which was built in 1852 and depicted in many Norman Rockwell paintings. It is said to be the most-photographed bridge in Vermont. The Bowers Bridge in Brownsville, built in 1919, was swept away but came to rest, mostly intact, downstream. The bridge on the Upper Cox Brook in Northfield Falls, Vermont, was impaled by a tree, but reopened in less than a week.

The Eunice Williams Bridge in Greenfield, Massachusetts only dates back to 1972, when it was rebuilt to replace a bridge that burned down, but it was built with quality materials in the old manner. When the Irene-swollen Green River tore its abutment away on one side, the bridge was left hanging over the river, so unstable that the town thought at first it would have to be torn down. With a little work, however, the loose end was secured, and now the town plans to rebuild it and make it strong enough for vehicles to use again, something the town hasn't enjoyed in a decade.

As this book goes to press, the Rockingham Town Board announced that the Worral Bridge would reopen in April after extensive repairs and the architectural firm of Clough Harbour & Associates had been hired to design the replacement for the Bartonsville Bridge. It will be slightly taller and larger than the original and will be the longest single span bridge in Vermont to be supported by a Ithiel Town truss, named after an American architect who patented the design in 1820. It was scheduled to open in the summer of 2012. ᥒ

10
Brattleboro, Vermont

A scenic brook that inspired artists becomes a killer;
A unique town worries about losing its artistic core.

The Whetstone Brook is the heart of the Brattleboro arts community. Its energetic waterfalls provide the motifs for hundreds of paintings and photographs, and its delicately rounded stones are transformed into the raw materials for sculptures and assemblies. The New England Youth Theater and the Latchis Theater, two of the town's centers for performance arts, flourish on its banks, and the Whetstone Studio for the Arts houses the working spaces for eight artists who can look out their windows at the babbling brook as it passes by.

So when Irene turned the Whetstone into a destroyer on August 28, it helps explain why Brattleboro took it so hard. It wasn't just a disaster; it was a betrayal by a trusted and loyal friend.

A town filled with art galleries and gift shops, Brattleboro is also home to a ballet studio, annual contra dances that last all night and into the next morning, an art nouveau movie theater, a bead store for craft workers, several pubs featuring live music and an annual morris dancing celebration that closes a main street and draws hundreds of spectators.

Ironically, the members of a local arts group called Brattleboro West Arts had planned an art exhibit called "Whetstone

243

Photo: Craig Brandon

This house, just off Route 9 in Marlboro, was flooded up to the second floor and cut off from the world when two bridges collapsed. In front of it flows the now calm Whetstone Brook.

Reflections," to celebrate the brook. Scheduled to open in early September, just a week after the flood, it was postponed but then reinstated with a new focus on the destruction caused by the brook and Irene. Naomi Lindenfield, a potter and one of the organizers of the event, said it was a way for local artists to express their feelings about what had happened.

Chris Lann created a necklace out of pebbles and roots collected from the brook that was designed to show the duel powers of the brook to move materials downstream while gravity held it in place. Ned Phoenix, the founder of the Estey Organ Museum, played a 25-minute piece he called Whetstone Waltz that he said reflected the rage of the water and the destruction it brought to Brattleboro as well as the friendly neighbor it has been during most of its 300-year relationship with the town. Potter Walter Slowinski built a miniature waterfall out of teapots and stones taken from the brook with water from the Whetstone flowing over them. His photos of the brook in various moods provided a backdrop for his sculpture.

Whetstone Falls, downtown near the theater just before the brook flows into the Connecticut, provided the power that created Brattleboro, the oldest town in Vermont, and became its industrial heart long before it became a haven for artists of every kind, a town full of art galleries, dance studios, unique gift shops and a popular bovine parade called "the strolling of the heifers." Brattleboro also has a knack for making the national news for the in-your-face attitudes of its citizens, including its refusal to ban public nudity and its indictment of President Bush and Vice President Cheney for war crimes. Mystery writer Archer Mayor is a local resident and sets his Joe Gunther stories in the town. John Villani's book *The 100 Best Small Art Towns in America* lists Brattleboro as number nine among towns with a population of 30,000 or under.

Even before Whetstone Brook began to overflow its banks on the morning of August 28, Brattleboro was already in disaster mode. A five-alarm downtown fire in April had turned a historic Main Street icon, the Brooks House, into a smoking shell. Then there was a series of murders, including one in which a manager shot another manager inside the Brattleboro Food Co-Op, another community center on the banks of the Whetstone.

They say bad news comes in threes, maybe that's why some residents were already preparing for another crisis, when weather maps showed Hurricane Irene with Brattleboro in her crosshairs, they just nodded and battened down the hatches, preparing for the worst.

Brattleboro, like other towns in the Irene Zone, endured the hours-long deluge as the storm stalled overhead, but the real

Photo: Ann Manwaring

The Marlboro Collision and Towing building, located between Route 9 and the Whetstone, collapses after the back of the building fell into the flooded brook.

damage began over a dozen miles away at the headwaters of the Whetstone, in the town of Marlboro, near the summit of Hogback Mountain. There the rain fell on the steep, saturated hillsides and merged into a massive flash flood wave that bounded down the steep hills along Vermont Route 9, heading straight for the heart of Brattleboro. Along the way it tore up the highway and carved out massive pieces of pavement that crashed down into the turbulent waters and were washed away. Cliffs, houses and bridges collapsed in turn and were swept along in the wave that only intensified as the slope of the hill became steeper. Picnic tables, cars, pieces of crushed houses and trees two-feet thick were carried down the stream. Boulders the size of small cars were dislodged from the streambed and rolled down the hill with a thud, thud sound that local residents said they would never forget. The mix of raging water and its shock wave of debris spilled out over the banks to crush any structure unlucky enough to be caught in the flow.

Among the early victims was the simple rectangular building that housed Marlboro Collision and Towing, a garage on a narrow strip of land between Route 9 and the Whetstone Brook that had been there for a dozen years. When the brook rose several feet in just a few minutes it eroded the north bank, where the building was located, and created a landslide on the other side. The combined force tore away the bank under the building and removed its foundation, eliminating in an instant the 150 yards that used to separate the building from the brook and leaving it precariously perched over the enlarged brook. Specialized tools and equipment fell through the floor and were washed away in the flood.

As the flood raced down the hill next to Route 9 it not only carved out pieces of the highway, but tore down bridges that crossed the brook, eliminating access to roads on the other side. At Cooke Road, for example, the concrete bridge deck that connected it to Route 9 was pulled down into the stream and the metal guardrails were twisted into a tangle. Tim Hamilton, who owns a sawmill and a maple sugar business on the other side, watched as some of his prime maple trees tipped over and fell into the brook. In an attempt to protect the bridge, he had placed dozens of half-ton concrete barricades and logs in the upstream path, but they were washed away in an instant. Hamilton, who was once a member of a research team that worked on an assessment of the Whetstone's corridor, knew what all that rain meant. A development boom along the Whetstone had infringed on the brook's floodplain and once it began to flood, he knew there was nowhere for all that water to go.

Photo: Randolph T. Holhut/The Commons

Flood-damaged mobile homes await removal at Brattleboro's Glen Park.

Photo: Chris Hart

The Whetstone Brook rushes through the Melrose Place public housing project on August 28.

Continuing on its mad flow to the east, the flash flood forged through the Mountain Home and Glen Street mobile home parks in West Brattleboro, where it pushed trailers off their foundations, washed away outbuildings and smashed through doors and windows, shoving furniture around and filling the homes with mud. Firemen tried to evacuate the 350-unit Mountain Home Park just after 10 a.m., but many of the residents were unable or unwilling to get out before it was too late as water raged all around them. The parts of Glen Street closest to the stream were evacuated, and firemen later advised the homes farther up the street to evacuate as well. Some sixteen of the trailers were so damaged that they were condemned as uninhabitable after water destroyed the electrical panels and plumbing.

Farther down the brook, dozens of brand new trailers and campers at the Vermont RV Sales and Service on Route 9 were washed away, many of them crashing into Paul Cannistraci's cleaning vans that were parked farther down the street. Both of them said they didn't know where to begin the cleanup. "Everything is completely gone," Gary Russell, the owner of the RV company, told the *Wall Street Journal*. "It's crazy. I can't even go to work," said Cannistraci.

After pushing the RVs around like billiard balls and destroying the trailers on Glen Street, the next stop for the raging waters was Melrose Place, a public housing project with eighty elderly and handicapped residents. It might have turned into a major tragedy except for one fact: no one was there. The day before, even before a drop of rain had fallen, in a move that may have saved multiple lives, Chris Hart, the executive director of the Brattleboro Housing Authority, had ordered the entire project evacuated.

"We met with the residents and got the bus ready, and the town and the Red Cross got the shelter ready at the high school," she said. "We told them to pack two days of medications. There were a lot of concerns about their cats and dogs so we went in and took care of them." When everyone was gone, she turned off the electricity. Many residents, of course, were reluctant to leave.

"Can you imagine telling couples in their mid 70s who had already been forced to leave their homes for public housing that they had to leave?" It was Hart's job to convince them that all hell was about to break loose on the shores of the Whetstone and later, when they were gone, she watched from her home on a nearby hill as the flood wave hit Melrose Place.

"The brook became a torrential river, just one angry huge waterway, two to three feet high" that divided into three streams as it left the Glen Street trailer park. Water pushed air conditioners out of the first story windows and rushed into the apartments. "There were propane tanks banging against the bridge," she said. "And I saw picnic tables, parts of mobile homes, huge logs rushing down, and the water rose up the sides of the brick housing units." Light poles and railings were knocked down and the water pushed a utility trailer down the stream where it broke into three pieces.

The next stop on the Whetstone's path was the Brattleboro Farmers' Market, a collection of wooden sheds used by local farmers and craftspeople to display their wares. The Whetstone usually made a wide circle around the sheds, but when the flood hit, it crashed right through, carrying the sheds, trees and a footbridge downstream, and the pieces eventually ended up in the Connecticut River. The stream gouged out large holes in the grassy field and deposited a thick layer of mud.

Pieces of the farmers' market buildings joined the wall of

Photo: Sarah Adam

A television film crew in front of the Whetstone Studio for the Arts on Williams Street in Brattleboro waits for the damaged rear of the building to collapse into the brook. After four days they went home.

picnic tables and mobile home parts making the steep descent through a gorge along Williams Street in Brattleboro, which was where the only Brattleboro casualty occurred. At 9:30 a.m. a resident called police to say he had seen a body floating in the Whetstone. The victim was later identified as Anthony "Tony" Doleszny, 52, father of two who lived on Marlboro Road. He had ridden his bicycle around several roadblocks on Williams Street and fell into a washed-out section of road. Water entered all the houses on the lower part of the street but saved its major force for the Whetstone Studio for the Arts, named, of course, for the tranquil stream that ran behind it.

Built about 1880 as a three-story warehouse and maintenance facility for the town's carriages and sleighs, the building had been empty for many years when David D. Parker, a local carpenter and devotee of the arts, renovated it to create a studio for eight local artists, including stained glass crafters, painters and sculptors. "I believe everything starts with the arts," Parker said. "Without the arts people's freedom of spirit and freedom of soul are not given the freedom to roam. I came from the coffeehouse era of Club 47 and Harvard Square, and I thought it was important for artists to have a place to go and an opportunity to share with other artists, sharing their aspirations and their dreams. I felt blessed to be connected with them and I wanted to give something back."

The building opened five years before the flood and was finally full during the summer of 2011 when Irene arrived. During the initial flash flood, Irene dug out the 70-foot foundation under the 130-year-old building, and the back of it tilted toward the stream, balancing precariously over the enlarged streambed. Parker's 1,600-square-foot workshop was in the bottom floor of that section. The floor collapsed and his tool collection, gathered over 40 years as a carpenter, fell into the Whetstone and was washed away.

"I lost all my workbenches, all my chisels, my hand planes, everything," he said. "All my machines went right down the brook. When I arrived on Monday morning everything was gone. The water came up 12 or 13 feet in a matter of minutes."

With less than a mile to go before the Whetstone entered the Connecticut River, the flood wave entered downtown

Photo: Sam's Outdoor Outfitters

Flat Street from Main Street in Brattleboro at the height of the flood on Sunday at noon. At the top is the Flat Street Parking Garage and to the left is the Latchis Building. The Brattleboro Boys and Girls Club is to the left of Sam's.

Photo: Sam's Outdoor Outfitters

Flat Street from the Parking Garage. The flooded area to the right covers two parking lots. At the top right is the Latchis Building and to the left is Sam's Outdoor Outfitters.

Brattleboro. Once again, the brook jumped out of its course to rush down Flat Street and cross over a parking lot. It finally returned to its banks to pass between the Latchis Theater and the Brattleboro Food Co-Op and flow under the Main Street Bridge and past the Amtrak Station.

Flat Street isn't really flat, but rises slightly before it reaches its terminus at Main Street, and that brief rise saved a number of businesses because instead of breaking out into Main Street, the major force of the stream was diverted through the Latchis parking lot and back within the Whetstone's normal bed. Nevertheless, the water crept up nearly to Main Street and the seeping water flowed under the doors of Flat Street businesses, flooding stores and warehouses and destroying millions of dollars worth of equipment, merchandise, carpets and flooring.

Caught in the main force was Sam's Outdoor Outfitters warehouse, where the Whetstone carried away some $10,000 worth of brand-new merchandise, including a number of canoes and kayaks that floated away down the Connecticut. Across the street, guests in the historic, 60-room Latchis Hotel, built in 1938 after the last hurricane, had to be evacuated to other hotels. Water entering through windows facing the brook filled the basement, climbed up to the third row of seats in the main theater and flooded the basement, shutting off the electricity. Windows at the back of the building, which are normally high above the Whetstone, became culverts that allowed water to fill the basements of the Latchis and the Flat Street Tavern and Brew Pub, which had a restaurant in the basement that was totally engulfed.

"I'd never seen anything like it before in my life," said Gail Nunziata, director of the Brattleboro Arts Initiative, which owns the Latchis. "It was just awful. We were all in our get-it-done mode. The first thing we did was evacuate all the guests and get them to remove their cars since the parking lot was right in the flood stream. Then we just watched the water. There was nothing else we could do. The water was coming in every opening in the building. It was just crazy."

The basement of the Emerson Furniture Store was flooded up to the rafters, destroying all the furniture that was stored there. Most of the businesses on Flat Street was flooded, although the

Photo: Craig Brandon

Bari Shamas, president of the board of directors of the New England Youth Theater, shows how the building's floodgates, installed at the bottom of the doors, kept out the damaging floodwaters.

severity of the damage varied. Water rushed into the Brattleboro Boys and Girls Club building on the north side, breaking the front windows and ruining carpets, the basketball court and kitchen equipment and covering everything with mud. The small shops and offices in the C.F. Church shopping center were flooded, including an optical shop, a home loan business and the county probate court. Across the street, Lynde Motorsports, a motorcycle repair shop, was also flooded.

Photo: Sam's Outdoor Outfitters

The grounds of the New England Youth Theater on Flat Street were covered with mud, but floodgates prevented any interior damage.

Photo: Peter Wilson

Water flows through a broken window into the basement of the Latchis Building, flooding the basement and the Flat Street Pub's restaurant.

But there was some good news as well. The campus of the New England Youth Theater was flooded outside, but the interior was mostly spared through the ingenious use of devices called "floodgates" that sealed off the doors preventing water from leaking in underneath them. The thin aluminum gates had originally been installed when the theater was constructed from former industrial buildings to comply with the town's floodplain rules.

The flood proofing, including the installation of concrete barriers on the side of the building nearest the Whetstone and the flood gates, 20-inch-high aluminum panels made to slip into slots on the door jam and seal out the water, saved the building. No one expected floodwaters to attack the building from the front; but when the Whetstone overran its banks, that was exactly what happened.

Bari Shamas, president of the board of directors, said that on Saturday night as Irene was approaching Vermont from the Atlantic, there had been a movie festival at the theater. When they were closing the theater down, Jerry Stockman, the building manager, decided to

Photo: Gail Nunziata

The main theater at the Latchis Building was flooded up to the third row of seats, but only minor damage resulted.

install the floodgates on the doors, something that had been done only once or twice before.

"It was a wonderful decision on his part," said Shamas, "and we all thanked him for it afterwards. There was a concern that someone might trip over them the next day, but we were certainly glad they were there."

Like the other buildings on that part of Flat Street, the theater was hit with a foot and a half of rushing water, but while it

Photo: Sarah Adam

For days after the flood, Flat Street was full of dumpsters being filled with debris.

flooded into the other buildings, it simply passed the theater by, and the only real inside damage was some ruined carpeting where the water rose over the gates.

"The water came down the street in ways that no one predicted," she said. "We always thought the water would come up from the back, where the brook was, but the gates protected us anyway." Needless to say, many of the other buildings on Flat Street have looked into the possibility of installing the gates in case another flood occurs.

The flash flood lasted only six hours. "Three hours for it to go up and three hours for it to go down," as Stanley "Pal" Borossky, owner of Sam's Outdoor Outfitters put it. But because police had blocked off the area, it wasn't until Monday morning that most shop owners got to see what was left. What hadn't been washed away was covered in six inches of smelly, shiny, clinging mud.

"It was definitely unhealthy," Pal said. Sam's shoe department, located on Flat Street, lost 7,000 pairs of shoes, many of them underwater. There was a big demand for rubber boots that week, of course, but he couldn't sell them because of the flooding. "We couldn't get to them."

The town brought in bulldozers that ran toward each other on Flat Street, scraping the mud into a pile that bucket loaders then dumped into trucks. "They did that over and over for days," recalled Nunziata. Every basement was full of water up to the first floor and had to be pumped out. It took Will Bissonette of

Photo: Gail Nunziata

Flood-damaged merchandise, including tablecloths, handbags and incense from the Adivasi Indian import shop on Flat Street is laid out in the sunshine to dry.

Photo: Sarah Adam

Cleaning trucks, dumpsters and fire trucks on Flat Street.

Photo: Sarah Adam

Flood debris fills the Latchis Building parking lot on Flat Street.

Photo: Craig Brandon

Whetstone Studio for the Arts, slightly shorter than before, being repaired in December.

the Flat Street Brew Pub an hour to force his way into what had been the downstairs restaurant to get to his basement office.

"The water was all gone but there was a foot of mud and everything had moved," he said, "all the kitchen equipment and all the tables and chairs. It was a complete disaster down there. I was in complete shock and awe of what six feet of water can do to a restaurant. It took most of the day to get back to the office. I pulled the cash out of the drawer, dried it off as best I could, and took it to the bank. The computers were all gone and all of our records. There was nothing to show that we even existed before the flood."

While the pub upstairs suffered only minor damage, it had to close because all the things it needed to operate—the walk-in coolers, the beer lines and all of its store products—were located in the basement. The pub didn't reopen until the week before Christmas, but Bissonette estimated that it would take another year before the restaurant could reopen.

The town moved dumpsters onto Flat Street to collect the ruined merchandise and equipment, and they stayed there for weeks as workers separated the mess, sorting the products that could be saved and sold at a flood sale from the ones that were ruined and had to be thrown out. Everything had to be dried out .and the thick mud had to be removed from buildings.

"This wasn't your garden-variety Connecticut Valley water," said Nunziata. "It was gooey gunk and it stank. It was slippery and it was treacherous." Once the water was pumped out of the basement, the Latchis brought in 22 refrigerator-sized dehumidifiers that went to work drying out the building and dumping the moisture into garbage-can-sized containers. But because the building's electric panels had been destroyed in the flood, a special power line had to be installed to run them. Seven weeks after the flood, the hotel and the theater were open for business and welcoming guests, but workers were still planning to install glass bricks to replace the open windows where the water had entered the building in August.

When David Parker arrived at the Whetstone Studio for the Arts on Monday and found the foundation gone, his workshop washed away and the building itself tilted backwards into the brook his first feeling was a tremendous sense of loss and despair.

"My mother's voice came to me in my head and told me to pick up your right foot and put it down and then pick up your left foot and put it down," he said. "It took me three days to pick up that second foot, but I kept going in the right direction. I thought I was functioning, but I can see now I was really in shock. I'm still grieving today because a lot of the stuff I had in my shop I'd had for over forty years. Stuff my children made when they were young. My granddaughter lost her toolbox. That stuff was irreplaceable, but in the end it was just stuff."

For the first four days after the flood, a television news crew was stationed nearby, waiting to film live when the back of the Whetstone studio collapsed into the brook. It never happened.

"I felt bad for them," said Parker. "They were here for four days and left disappointed."

Photo: Luke Q. Stafford

Whetstone Brook is over its banks and almost up to this balcony as it makes its final descent into the Connecticut River.

Meanwhile he hired a work crew to rebuild the studio, a little shorter than it used to be so it didn't hang out over the brook, but right in the same spot. Work was still underway at the beginning of 2012, and Parker hoped to move his artists back in soon, including several new ones who want to be a part of his Whetstone community.

The total cost of the damage on Flat Street alone was estimated in the multiple millions of dollars including damage to buildings, lost income and ruined goods. At Adivasi, an Indian import store on the south side of Flat Street in the Latchis building, owner Meyu Bhanti and her family spread colorful tablecloths, packages of incense and napkins out in the street and in the Latchis parking lot in an effort to dry them in the sun and save as much as they could.

Meanwhile, Cooke Road residents found they were cut off from the outside world and had to use a six-foot stepladder to descend into the steambed and then traverse stout planks to walk across to Route 9. Tim Hamilton had to chainsaw and winch his prime maple trees out of the brook, but even if they could rig up a temporary bridge, they could not go anywhere because of the jagged hole just to the west where Route 9 should

Photo: Sarah Adam

Volunteers use a hose and rags to clean the mud from furniture after the water receded on Flat Street.

have been. It would be a few days before the highway and the bridge were back in order.

All along the Whetstone, residents found debris that had been torn from houses upstream: bathroom sinks, photo albums, golf clubs, china cups, children's dolls and teddy bears. Houses that had not been swept away were full of toxic mud and the sheetrock had to be removed quickly before it became contaminated with mold. When residents returned to the Mountain Home Trailer Park, they found it covered in silt and mud, like low tide on a beach. Outbuildings had been smashed and lawn mowers, tools and propane tanks full of expensive gas were gone or empty. Cars had been smashed against buildings.

Things were no better on Glen Street, where some of the mobile homes had been shifted twenty feet from their foundations and many had their sides bashed in. Residents entered their former homes to save what they could, transferring items to their cars.

Photo: Craig Brandon
David Parker at the newly rebuilt Whetstone Studio for the Arts.

On Monday the remaining residents began hauling out their furniture, tools, clothing and appliances so they could dry out in the sun. Sixteen of the trailers were immediately condemned by the state as unfit for habitation, but residents complained they had nowhere to go and couldn't afford to rent a new place. Later in the week, as the mud began to dry, dust clouds full of the toxic mud from the flood began to choke the residents as they continued their salvage work.

Across the brook at Melrose Place, residents of the few second story apartments began to move in almost immediately, since the buildings were found to be structurally sound. Many of the ground-floor apartments were severely flooded and there were five and six inches of mud on the floors and carpets and sheetrock needed to be replaced. And then there was the smell.

"Melrose Place smelled like a gas refinery," Hart said. "That water went through farms and mobile home parks before it got here. It was really horrid stuff. The volunteers had gloves and masks on, and we asked them to wash their boots when they got home." The housing authority brought in large pod containers so residents could store their belongings while workers rebuilt their apartments. Many of their belongings, however, were ruined and ended up in the dumpsters. By the end of the year there were still twenty residents who had not been able to return.

"Many of these people had lost things that were important to them: their furniture, their knitting. Their family photos were soaked. It was very difficult," Hart said.

The Paquette brothers, owners of Marlboro Collision and Towing, thought at first that they could salvage their building, which was now perched precariously over the Whetstone Brook, but eight days later, after more rain, the main beam cracked and the building split down the middle, now a total loss. By the end of the year, an entirely new building was being completed on the site of the old one, now a lot closer to the highway than it used to be because the streambed is so much wider. The Boys and Girls Club reopened just 11 days after the flood with the help of over 100 volunteers and a $50,000 grant from Entergy, the company that owns a nearby nuclear power plant.

While the Whetstone Brook got all the attention during the storm because it flowed through the middle of Brattleboro, Irene washed out roads and destroyed homes and bridges in nearly every part of Windham County. The Grafton Fire Department had to rescue a woman who was clinging to a tree in the middle of the Saxtons River after her car got stuck and washed away on Route 121.

Parts of Route 100, the main north and south road in central Vermont, and Route 30 were washed out in dozens of places and communities were cut off when bridges collapsed. Unwilling to wait for town and state highway crews, local excavating companies went to work on their own attempting to rebuild collapsed roads and in some cases even carve new roads to bypass the washed-out sections.

The Marlboro Branch River, for example, carved a deep canyon down the middle of Augur Hole Road in South Newfane. On Monday, after the water receded, residents were cut off from each other and the remains of the road looked like a creek bed. Residents couldn't call for help because their phone lines

Photo: Luke Q. Stafford

Construction was a common sight during the fall of 2011, such as this scene on Dover Road in South Newfane.

were down and emergency workers couldn't get there anyway because so many bridges were unsafe and there was no road to drive on.

Resourceful New Englanders like Willie Schroeder and Rory Lincoln used their all-terrain vehicles to travel from house to house, checking on residents, delivering water and food and bringing in the news from the outside world. In some cases the residents were located as many as six miles from the nearest working road, but the vehicles were able to negotiate the ruined roads and the new stream beds. The roar of chainsaws filled the air as residents cleared fallen trees out of their driveways.

Residents with their own heavy equipment started the huge task of rebuilding the roads so residents could get out and emergency vehicles could get in. In some cases entirely new roads had to be carved out of the forest to get to people who were cut off by the collapsed roads.

Local farmers lost all or part of their crops and suffered from damaged barns and equipment. Cory Walker of Guerrilla Grown Produce in Westminster said he lost all of his winter crops, half of his total income for the year. Over five acres of vegetables had to be destroyed because they came in contact with the toxic floodwater. Paul Dutton of Dutton's Berry Farm in Newfane said he depended on tourists during leaf-peeping season and he worried that unless the roads could be rebuilt soon he would lose all that business. As it was, he lost fields full of chrysanthemums and 300 small fruit trees that were picked up and carried away. Also flooded and lost were fields full of tomatoes, watermelons, cantaloupe, zucchini and squash.

When residents finally returned to their homes days after the waters receded, they found them unrecognizable. Those that had managed to remain intact were closer to the rivers and streams than they had been before, some balanced on eroding stream banks. The tall trees that used to line the watercourses were gone, replaced by piles of uprooted trees, huge boulders and thick layers of silt along the streams that now looked like beaches.

For many of the residents of Melrose Place, life would never return to normal, Chris Hart said. "A lot of people have difficulty every time it rains. Fear takes over. There's no way any of our residents are going to have to go through this again. There are alternatives, but it is going to take us a year or so to come up with a plan."

David Parker said Brattleboro's response to the flood only underscored why it was the kind of community in which he wanted to live. "I feel blessed living here because all of us came together that day. It's a tremendous community." ✑

11
Aftermath

When the rain ended, the recovery began, but getting back to "normal" remained an elusive goal.

When her eight hours of devastation were over, Irene made a smooth getaway back out over the Atlantic and diminished into a low pressure area before finally disappearing forever. Her name was officially retired, but for the shocked residents of the Irene Zone, her name is not likely to ever be forgotten.

It wasn't until the waters receded and the bright sunshine dawned on Monday morning, August 29 that Irene Zone residents got a good look at the unbelievable devastation. In places like Pratttsville, New York, the entire town looked like it had been shelled by an artillery barrage. In places like Waterbury and Schoharie, the visible damage was only a prelude to the much more significant water damage that turned hundreds of houses into black mold incubators.

Shocked residents who had been evacuated overnight woke up in cots in schools and community centers, ready to go home, only to be carefully informed that "home" was uninhabitable and they should plan to stay with neighbors or in a motel for the foreseeable future. Many first saw their ruined homes and businesses on YouTube videos.

Mud was everywhere, one to six inches of brown, gooey,

Photo: Luke Q. Stafford

On Monday morning in South Newfane, life went on even with half the street gone.

smelly stuff with the texture of Jell-O that resisted all efforts to shovel it into trash cans. It just ran off their shovels until workers understood that the best technique was to push it up a ramp and down into a bucket. Everyone who worked with it came to realize it was a lot more than just "mud"—it contained farm chemicals, heating oil, propane residue and sewage. Best not to think about that.

When it dried out towards the end of the week it turned into a toxic dust that mixed with the mold that was already forming on surfaces in the hot August sun. Face masks became fashion accessories among the cleanup crews, along with their official tools: mops, buckets and sledge hammers. Many residents took their $30,000 FEMA checks and left town, leaving others to clean up the mess.

Sweat equity was plentiful as neighbors went to work to put their towns back together and help arrived from faraway states, ready to lend a hand. The National Guard directed traffic and blocked off highways as road crews began the hard work of dumping tens of thousands of tons of rock into the deep voids that Irene had carved in the highway systems of three states. Despite the incredible and widespread damage, all the major highways in the Irene Zone were restored by the end of the year.

For businesses that were already troubled by the recession, Irene was often the final straw that led their owners to close their doors for good. The difficulties were just insurmountable. Other businesses sprang back almost immediately, supported by loans and savings and mounds of debt. Finding the money for repairs and restocking the shelves became a difficult matter of figuring out which form to fill out, where to send information. Even simple questions like should I repair the damage immediately or wait for the insurance inspector seemed not to have any ready answers.

Six months later, throughout the Irene zone, damaged and boarded-up houses and shops abound. The main streets of Schoharie and Prattsville were ghost towns, and in Waterbury businesses waited to find out if those 1,500 state workers were gone for good. In Williamstown's Spruces Mobile Home Park, scores of ruined trailers were still lined up in rows waiting for a resolution. In Brattleboro, there were few signs that the flood had occurred at all, but places like the Latchis Theater were still looking for donations to pay for all the repairs. In Wilmington, a community non-profit was buying up damaged historic buildings and looking for new tenants to fill them.

Hovering in the background, because New Yorkers and New Englanders were reluctant to talk about it, was the question of money. Making repairs is one thing, but who is going to pay the millions of dollars in damages? FEMA did its part for home owners, and states, and federal government agencies were generous with businesses and local governments, but it was clear six months later that many millions of dollars were still required before things could return to anything resembling "normal."

Meanwhile, experts in engineering, zoning, planning, flood control and disaster preparedness were drawing up reports about what worked and what didn't and what could be changed to improve the situation next time—because there would certainly be a next time.

First of all, towns and even states had to rethink where they located their emergency control centers. In Charlemont, Massachusetts, the fire station, located near the banks of the Deerfield River, quickly flooded. The State of Vermont learned that the state offices in Waterbury, located in a floodplain, was not a good choice either. Both of those locations have been revised.

Next on the list was the whole idea of what was and what was not a "floodplain." Before Irene, planners referred to a "hundred-year flood zone" as the maximum area that could be expected to be underwater in a worst-case scenario. Within that area

Photo: Ann Manwaring

In Wilmington, the arrival of National Guard troops and heavy vehicles added to the nightmarish sense of unreality.

there were restrictions on development to protect buildings and the surrounding area. During Irene, however, properties were flooded that were miles from any official floodplain. Houses on cliffs fifty feet high and fifty feet back from a stream were pulled into rivers. Covered bridges that had withstood floods for a century and a half were pulled down and destroyed.

At the very least, new rules were being put in place to prevent trailer parks from setting up shop in floodplains and FEMA refused to help anyone to rebuild a house located in a designated floodplain. Some residents who were rebuilding their houses built them on stilts or with an empty first story and a home that began on the second story. Road engineers increased the size of the culverts under highways so they would not clog in a major storm, one of the prime reasons for highway failure during Irene.

Hydraulic engineers began speaking about a "five-hundred year flood" and coming up with new maps. The problem was that five hundred years before Irene, in 1511, there were no weather records being kept, no bridges or highways and the Native Americans who lived in what is now New England and New York simply moved to higher ground when the waters rose. And if it really was a disaster that could be expected every 500 years, did it make sense in 2012 to prepare for another storm in 2511?

Related to all this planning was the idea that the bizarre weather of 2011 and 2012 was more than just a random occurrence and might be the result of man-made climate change, the consequence of releasing too much carbon dioxide into the atmosphere, creating a green house effect that trapped heat. The heat melted glaciers and permafrost and reduced the area of the Arctic that was free from ice, all factors that could have an impact on climate and create the conditions that caused Irene.

Mary Watzin, dean of the University of Vermont's School of Environment and National Resources said climate models show that New England can expect a 61 percent increase in severe storms during the next decades. Rivers, she said, need room to run with the least interference possible. Attempts to straighten river channels prevent rivers from meandering and increase their flow rate, increasing the potential for disasters when they flood.

A controversy has erupted throughout the Irene Zone about whether heavy equipment was properly used to clear out streambeds clogged with rocks, trees and debris from the storm. In Brattleboro, for example, some property owners began building berms along the Whetstone Brook to protect them in future storms, but downstream property owners who did not have protection worried that these measures would make it worse for them the next time. This "stream armoring," as it is called, was widely discouraged by experts taking the long view, but property owners felt it was a natural instinct to protect themselves from another Irene.

In Vermont, Massachusetts and New York, the strict environmental rules that prohibit streambed work without a permit were temporarily suspended by their governors. Dredging a riverbed to make the channel deeper and remove gravel that washed down in the storm can make rivers run faster and therefore cause more damage during future storms. Much of the gravel dredged up from rivers immediately after the storm was used to rebuild highways. In other words, work crews were putting back into the roads the same rocks that had been washed away.

During testimony at the Vermont State House in November, environmentalists said dredging streams for fill was a sign of shoddy restoration work. David Mears, commissioner of the State Department of Environmental Conservation, said "spending money to do work without consideration for how river dynamics work is just money down the hole. We're just going to replace the same culverts, the same bridges the same homes, the same roads over and over again if we don't do it right."

Ron Rhodes, a river steward at the Connecticut River Watershed Council, said unchecked dredging and channelizing in an attempt to "fix" rivers was a failed practice of the past and should be prohibited, even during an emergency.

Richard Tetreault, chief engineer of the Vermont Agency of Transportation, said Irene washed out more than 2,000 highway segments, undermined more than 1,000 culverts and damaged more than 300 bridges. The roads that survived the storm best, he said, were the highly engineered interstates and the "super Route 7" south of Burlington.

"As we both rebuild from flood damage and replace aging bridges over time," he said, "we need to rethink their design. In the past, we built relatively short bridges with concrete abutments close to, if not in, rushing water. These designs were cost-effective and made environmental sense at the time. The time has now come, however, to consider building longer bridges with foundations that sit outside our river channels, even if these bridges cost more and have a longer footprint."

Communities, he said, will have to come up with new answers to questions like how close to the water is too close to build. This land is often attractive to home owners because of

Photo: Luke Q. Stafford

In Southern Vermont, once-familiar streams become moonscapes with freshly disturbed boulders, heavy equipment parts and even smashed cars.

Photo: Luke Q. Stafford

Slopes collapsed onto roads and bridges and debris of all kinds washed up against roadways, including trees, appliances, concrete blocks and parts of buildings. Boulders filled stream beds to the brim.

its scenic value, but Irene showed that too many houses were built too close to riverbanks. When more water capacity is required during heavy rains, he said, rivers need access to their floodplains so the excess water in the confined channel does not increase in energy and destructive capacity, blowing out roads, houses and bridges downstream.

When residents and taxpayers asked about the possibility of future Irenes, the issue became connected to the controversy over climate change. If the climate is changing, we can no longer use the past to predict the future but must prepare for the unknown. Is the climate changing?

The answer is yes, according to Michael Rawlins, manager of the University of Massachusetts Climate System Resource Center. We need to plan for more severe weather events, he said, with more tropical storms and more of the kind of intense precipitation that devastated the Irene Zone.

"When we talk implementing plans, do we really know what we are designing for?" he asked a meeting of planners from the extensively damaged Deerfield River watershed in March 2012. "Let's not lose sight that there's a large uncertainty in what we can expect over the next few decades as far as extreme events." The meeting was attended by fifty planners who said they were overwhelmed and unprepared when Irene attacked them.

"There's a huge disconnect. We just don't have the ability to deal with this, given our political boundaries," said Carolyn Shores Ness, the Deerfield selectman who attended the meeting. "How do we get our beautiful, wild rivers back" but still maintain roads and bridges? It was a question for which there are no easy answers.

Orin Langelle of Hinesville, Vermont, board chair for Global Justice Ecology Project in Vermont, said a combination of factors made it obvious that severe climate change was occurring. On the last day of winter in 2012 the temperature was 81 degrees and iceout on Lake Iroquois was arriving earlier each year.

"This year on Saint Patrick's day in mid-March, people were water skiing instead of cross-country skiing," he said. "Many of us did not go snowshoeing or cross-country skiing this winter. There just wasn't enough snow. Compare that to last spring, when the rapid thaw of late-winter snow caused record flooding around the state, with homes on Lake Champlain and farms along the rivers devastated by the high water. This year the lack of snow and rain has left the forests tinder dry and fire warnings have been issued.

"March is normally Vermont's big month for maple syrup production," he said. "This year the weather has been too warm. The maple trees are moving north and in fifty years there may be no more sugaring in Vermont. In the aftermath of Irene, the next day in fact, my wife, Anne and I photographed and interviewed military personnel from Camp Johnson in Essex, where the National Guard was mobilizing and FEMA was beginning to arrive. We ended up later that day on Route 100 headed toward Grafton, one of the towns cut off due to washed-out roads. We went as far as we could go before a collapsed roadbed blocked us.

"Between going to Camp Johnson and winding up at the washed-out road near Grafton, we spent the day in Waterbury. As you can see from my photos, most of Waterbury was just beginning to recover from Irene. People who lost everything were helping each other. Volunteers were pouring in. The community was coming together.

"Was Irene caused by the changing climate? To me, quite certainly, but in the end it is up to you to decide. Many of the pundits reading news on TV and radio like to talk about "100-year storms," but how many years of 100-year storms and floods do we need before we understand they are becoming the norm?

A recent report from the Union of Concerned Scientists reported that, "recent scientific evidence suggests a link between the destructive power (or intensity) of hurricanes and higher ocean temperatures, driven by global warming. It is evident to many of us that for far too long industrial civilization has been belching carbon into the atmosphere. It is too late to stop the damage that has already been done. But maybe we can head off more damage before it gets much worse if we take the problem seriously and begin to address it now."

"It is a shame though that it takes disaster for most people in communities to work hand in hand for their common good," said Langelle. "Maybe it is time for real community to come together—not just after a disaster hits—but all of the time. Maybe then we can find the real solutions that can prevent the disasters in the first place."

Another long-term impact on the Irene Zone is the new landscape the storm created. Many of the tree-lined rivers and streams so popular on Vermont tourist post cards are gone and replaced with eroded banks, treeless shores and "beaches" formed by silt washed down by Irene. Many streams now feature eroded cliffs hundreds of feet high. While the silt can be removed inside community limits, it is likely to remain in rural areas for decades. Some areas along formerly flooded streams look like moonscapes full of boulders and sand.

One of the more difficult problems in the Irene Zone is the psychological damage inflicted on the survivors, the post-traumatic stress disorder, depression and nightmares that are the human toll of dealing with disaster. Many of the survivors interviewed for this book told their stories bravely and forcefully, but at some point many of them broke down in tears and could not go on. What triggered this was usually something relatively minor: a blogger chastising them for their failure to buy health insurance or a family photo lost in the flood. Sometimes it was the thought of a pet that was lost.

One common complaint we heard over and over was a fear of rainfall. Parents said their children cried whenever it rained and asked them if they were going to have to move again, but adults as well said that whenever it looked like rain, there was the urge to run away to higher ground. Months after the disaster, many children could not talk about what had happened to their homes, their toys and their friends. At Moretown Elementary School in Vermont, students were disrupted for months while their school was dried out with industrial dehumidifiers. They had to sit on blue tarps on the baseball field, singing "You Can't Keep A Good Town Down," while environmental service crews worked inside the building.

A special puppet show for flood-impacted towns in Vermont was organized by Karen Sharpwolf and Karen Newman of Burlington. It encouraged students to share their feelings about what had happened to them and why. Elderly survivors in places like the Spruces in Williamstown and the community-supported housing in Brattleboro seemed to have only a minimal understanding about what had happened to their homes and their community.

Cathy Aikman, project director of Starting Over Strong (SOS), a FEMA-sponsored program that offers mental health counseling for flood victims, said dealing with these problems was an important part of the recovery. Many survivors are suffering from post-traumatic stress disorder. SOS set up regular focus groups in flood-impacted towns where survivors could talk about their problems and share solutions. Among the symptoms SOS encountered were frequent and sudden tearfulness, feeling numb, withdrawn or disconnected; and trouble sleeping or nightmares about storms or floods.

Sonja Hakala, an Irene survivor from West Hartford, Vermont, described for Vermont Public Radio what it was like after the flood. "You feel like you have woken up in someone else's nightmare," she said. "This is where you live, this is your home, but everything has shifted under your feet." Before Irene, she said, she considered the river a lovely part of nature. Now, she said, she no longer trusts the river. When it rains, she gets nervous and watches it carefully.

Kevin Buchanan, medical director of the Clara Martin Center in Vermont, said the stress system of survivors of storms like Irene can go into overdrive causing a variety of emotional and physical symptoms that gradually go away, but can be triggered again by rain storms.

Mame McKee of Rebuild Waterbury, who has spoken with nearly 200 survivors, said many of them had not yet begun to emotionally process what had happened to them.

"Everybody whose life has changed has a different perspective," she said. "There is a deep psychological impact and things will never be the same. People need to tell their stories. They need to cry a bit." ᜰ

How You Can Help

From the very first day of the storm, volunteers and charities set up shop to help the survivors. Volunteer work and contributions are still desperately needed. Here is where you can get more information about how you can help:

Schoharie Recovery, Inc. PO Box 111 Schoharie, NY 12157 (518) 390-828 www.schoharierecovery.org

Schoharie Area Long Term (SALT) PO Box 777 Schoharie, NY 12157 (518) 702-5017 www.saltrecovery.org

Fields of Grace PO Box 48 Middleburgh, NY 12122 (518) 827-5344 www.fieldsofgraceoutreach.org

Puppets in Education (shows for children victims) (802) 860-3349   www.puppetsineducation.org

Vermont Response www.vtresponse.wordpress.com/tag/hurricane-irene/ vtresponse@yahoo.com

Rebuild Waterbury PO Box 633 Waterbury VT 05676 (802) 793-7182   www.rebuildwaterbury.com

Wilmington Small Business www.wilmingtonVTfloodrelief.com

Waterbury Good Neighbor Fund www.waterburyucc.org

Weston Playhouse Theater Co. 703 Main Street, WestonVT. 05161

Vermont Small Business Owners, www.vtirenefund.org/donate

Pittsfield Vt, www.pittsfieldhurricanerelief.org

282   Craig Brandon, Nicole Garman, Michael Ryan

Vermont Farm Diaster Relief Fund www.vermontcf.org/give-now

I Am Veront Strong www.iamvermontstrong.com

Scene Shop Challenge, Williamstown Theater Festival PO Box 517, Williamstown Mass., 01267

Shelburne Falls Area Business Association's West County Relief Fund at www.shelburnefalls.com.

Higher Ground, 906 Main Street, Williamstown MA 01267 (413) 458-4237 www.nbhighergrund.org

Dot's Restaurant, Wilmington Vt   www.Rebuilddots.com

I am Vermont Strong www.iamvermontstrong.com

The Wilmington Vermont Fund - www.the wilmingtonvtfund.org

Prattsville Relief Fund c/o NBT Bank P.O Box 380 Grand Gorge, NY 12434

Contributors

Good Night Irene would not have been possible without the many hours of hard work by these people:

Craig Brandon, *author, photographer and editor*, is a national award-winning author of seven books and an award-winning former newspaper reporter. His day job is editor and publisher of Surry Cottage Books.

Nicole Garman *co-author and photographer* (Vermont) is a writer, designer, and snowboarder. Her work has appeared everywhere from magazines to psychic websites, and she thanks the 802 for every tear.

Michael Ryan *co-author, photographer* (Catskills) won an Associated Press award for his coverage of Irene for the *Windham Journal*. He lives on a dead end road in the Catskills and has Druid blood in his veins as well as a playful passion for words thanks to his father and mother.

Luke Q. Stafford *blogger and photographer* (southern Vermont) is a writer, photographer, web page designer and founder of Mondo Media Works in Brattleboro, Vermont. www.mondomediaworks.com

Ann Manwaring, *photographer* (Wilmington) is a Democratic Vermont state legislator representing Wilmington. She has a very impressive collection of photos from the Irene disaster that she took while assisting her constituents in their hours of need.

Sarah Adam, *photographer* (Brattleboro) is an illustrator and graphic designer living in Brattleboro. She enjoys painting and photography as a means of expression and documenting the world around her. You can see more of her work at Madsahara.com or visit her on Facebook.

Orin Langelle *photographer* (Waterbury) is the board chair for the Global Justice Ecology Project and is a photojournalist now editing four decades of his photography.

Also:
Lars Gange, *photographer* (Vermont)
Nancy Nutlie-McEnemy, *photographer* (Vermont)
John Redd, *photographer* (Wilmington)

Acknowledgments

Craig Brandon would like to express gratitude to his tolerant and ever-fascinating wife, Jean Winter, who is the perfect writer's spouse. She was never jealous, not even for a moment, when she heard her husband was spending all his time with a wild and crazy femme fatale named Irene. Next come my talented and dependable co-authors, Nicole Garman and Mike Ryan, who came through countless times, despite my unrealistic expectations about deadlines, nearly restoring my faith in freelance writers. Elaine Ambrose is Surry Cottage Books' wizard of proof reading and copy editing. We would be lost without her. This book would have been impossible without the scores of amateur and professional photographers who gave us access to their hard drives and let us take our pick of their Irene collections. We didn't use any photos from people who wanted to charge us $500 per picture! Essential to us was the work of Sarah Adam, Orin Langelle, Ann Manwaring, Nancy Nutlie-McEnemy, John Redd and Lars Gange. A special thanks to all the wonderful FEMA photographers, especially Hans Pennink, who took our cover photo. Thanks to FEMA itself for letting us use all those great photos!

During hundreds of miles of travels in three states for this book, we encountered hundreds of Irene survivors with stories to tell and I wish I could thank each one of them. I hope you found us to be good listeners! Specials thanks to, in no particular order, Phil Camp, Ed Smith, Rachel Porter, Nina Brennan, Leslie Price, Josh DeBartolo, Mame McKee, Jason Dalley, Lisa Sullivan, Ken Gillette, Luke Q, Stafford, Anne Ashmeade, David Parker, Gail Nunziata, and Larry Syzdek. I am also grateful to my teacher, friend and fellow author Campbell Black, who lives a continent away but remains close by e-mail.

Nicole Garman writes: I have learned so much on the *Goodnight Irene* project, and I would like to thank every single person who's lent a hand along the way. Vern and Patty Haskins, Rhianna Graham-Frock and her friends, Heather Gorton, Amy Zajdel, Justin Laramie, the amazingly friendly folks at the Bridgewater Mill and Woodstock Farmers' Market, John and Jen Kimmich and the team at The Alchemist, the staff at Juniper's Fare, Brian Halligan, Nina Brennan, the good people at Killington Resort, and so many more who've shared their stories. The strength and warmth of Vermonters is truly incredible; thank you to the people of Woodstock, Bridgewater, West Bridgewater, Rutland, Killington, Pittsfield, Waterbury, Bethel, Northfield, Rochester, and beyond for welcoming me into your lives, businesses, and homes. Thank you to the friends, family, neighbors, and coworkers who've gone out of their way and taught me about writing, Vermont, and living fiercely—it's been an adventure.

Michael Ryan would like to thank 150-year-old *Windham Journal* editor Lori Anander for being the best boss ever. Anander published the weekly newspaper without missing a beat as the events of Tropical Storm Irene unfolded around her, and somehow tolerates me (the *Windham Journal* is a century-and-a-half old, not Anander. I regret any confusion). Thanks go to Kory O'Hara and the Young family for sharing their stories. The writer wishes to thank town of Prattsville administrative assistant Michele Brainard, town of Ashland administrative assistant Diane Cross, Windham town historian Patricia Morrow, Pratt Museum Director Carolyn Bennett, Windham town clerk Carolyn Garvey, Lexington town clerk Rose Williams, Jewett town supervisor Carol Muth, blossoming curmudgeon Jim Planck, Delaware Engineering eclectic John Brust and Hudson-Catskill Newspapers publisher Roger Coleman and executive director Theresa Hyland for their help, support and kindness. The writer also wishes that the late T. Patrick Meehan had not left so soon.

Index

Before and after: Anastasia Rikard's beautiful three-story, Victorian house in Prattsville, New York, as it looked before August 28, (above) and after Irene ran the Schoharie Creek through it (below). The house was on the front page of the New York Times *and served as a backdrop for dozens of TV news reports. Its final demise is recorded on the cover of this book.*

A woman in Waterbury, Vermont spreads a wet towel out to dry after Tropical Storm Irene forced the Winooski River to overflow its banks into a residential area.

The remains of the historic Bartonsville Covered Bridge along the shore of the Williams River in Rockingham County, Vermont. The collapse of the bridge was caught on video and posted on YouTube. The town plans to rebuild the bridge using some of this wreckage.

Photo: Angela Drexel (FEMA)
A house in Bethel, Vermont is pulled off its foundation, leaving only the second story.

Photo: Wendell Davis (FEMA)

The owners of the house salvaged some of their belongings in the front yard.

Jim McGrath, a Wilmington, Vermont, watercolor artist, painted this during the storm. It's called "From my Window."

Disc Jockies Sonny Rock (L) and Joe Loverro (R) from WRIP 97.7 broadcast from the Command Center on Main Street in Prattsville NY. They encouraged people to volunteer in the New York State "Labor for your neighbor" campaign which is helping those impacted by the flooding caused by Irene.

Photo: Lars Gange

The National Guard protects a dangerous section of Vermont highway that was washed out by Irene. Soldiers are visible at the top section of highway while an Army bulldozer works at the bottom right.

Photo: Elissa Jun (FEMA)

Even Old Glory was not immune from Irene's wrath as shown here with a pile of debris collected on a street in Schoharie, New York.

What to save and what to toss was a difficult decision for Irene survivors. Most possessions had be tossed. Here, on a muddy yard, a Schoharie New York resident has spread items to be saved on a tarpaulin.

This house on Collier Road on the Schoharie Creek in Burtonsville, New York, was directly in the path of the flood. The swollen creek waters passed through the building carrying appliances and household goods.

Photo: Sarah Adam

The warm sunny days after August 28 were perfect for cleaning up all over the Irene Zone. The Adivasi import store on Flat Street in Brattleboro Vermont had some of the most interesting items to clean.

Volunteers took advantage of the fact that Flat Street was closed to spread out all kinds of tablecloths, incense, picture frames and journals on the pavement to dry out in the sunshine.

No one expected the high lodge at Killington, Vermont to be flooded. Irene tore the building apart and pushed this truck into a brand new ravine. Because the roads were cut off there was no way in or out of the resort and one guest chartered a helicopter to escape.

Photo: Lars Gange

This house in Rochester, Vermont was destroyed not by the White River, but by a flooded stream that rushed down at right angles.

Photo: Adam DuBrowa (FEMA)

Muddy clothing is hung on trees outside this damaged house in Prattsville, New York.

Photo: Lars Gange

Irene's path of destruction in Vermont can be seen in this photo taken from the air. A stream overflowed at the top left and eroded the highway before spreading out at the bottom of the photo.

The Mohawk Trail, Massachusetts, at the Charlemont - Savoy border.

Filling in all the road washouts in Vermont required tens of thousands of tons of gravel, which had to be brought in by railroad cars.

Photo: Eric Dean

The driver of this car had to be rescued after the car almost fell into this sink hole in Charlemont, Mass.

Photo: Angela Drexel (FEMA)

Steve Wright's Stone House in Woodford, Vermont. (see chapter 4.)